N. W. Fink

THE BOOK OF JOB:
ITS SUBSTANCE AND SPIRIT

THE MACMILLAN COMPANY
NEW YORK · BOSTON · CHICAGO · DALLAS
ATLANTA · SAN FRANCISCO

MACMILLAN & CO., Limited
LONDON · BOMBAY · CALCUTTA
MELBOURNE

THE MACMILLAN COMPANY
OF CANADA, Limited
TORONTO

THE BOOK OF JOB:
ITS SUBSTANCE AND SPIRIT

BY

W. G. JORDAN, B.A., D.D.

PROFESSOR OF HEBREW LITERATURE, QUEEN'S UNIVERSITY
KINGSTON, ONTARIO

NEW YORK
THE MACMILLAN COMPANY
1929

TO MY FRIEND

LORNE PIERCE, LL.D., F.R.S.C.

*in recognition of his services on behalf of good
literature and especially the zeal that he has
shown in appreciating and encouraging literary activity in this great Dominion*

PREFACE

At this stage it may seem unnecessary to send out another volume, even a small one, on the Book of Job. The excuse must be that this book does not expect to take the place of any of the commentaries and critical discussions that have gathered round these remarkable poems. I have had, as a part of the work of preparation, to read the Hebrew text, in some passages a painful process, and to take note of what scholars have done in this field. Such special studies do not reach a large number of people, and there should be room for another attempt to present the spirit and substance of the book without going too far into technical questions of translation and exegesis. Two things will probably be admitted by those who have given any attention to the subject; first, the immense amount of research spent upon it by scholars in ancient and modern times, and, second, the comparative neglect of it by ordinary readers of the Bible. If the second of these facts is accounted for by the form in which the book has been handed down to us by Jewish scribes it may be possible to give help by a re-arrangement of the material. The reasons for this will be given briefly in the first section where questions will be discussed that cannot be evaded in the study of an ancient book. In the second section what we regard as the original book will be presented with brief connecting comments. The third will, without going into the minute study of texts and

7

marginal notes, consist of poems which are now
regarded by many scholars as coming from different
hands and a later time.

It is as a great literary work that we desire to present it, but the theological significance and religious
spirit instead of being suppressed will, we hope, thereby
find a richer expression. This is becoming clearer the
more the Bible is studied in the light of fuller knowledge now available as to the life of the Hebrew people
and the nature of their literature. There are people
who demur to the study of the Bible as literature on
the ground that the Word of God should be spared this
kind of examination. "The best reason for studying
the Bible as literature is that it *is* literature. The
Books of the Bible have every characteristic of literature, and in the course of time they have been subject
to all the adventures and misadventures which beset
literary documents." [1] This has long been known to
students of the history and the language but, in more
popular forms, it is now attracting the attention of the
general public.

Speaking of the past, Professor G. M. Trevelyan
said, in his Inaugural Address: [2] "The common people,
it is true, only shared indirectly in the classical culture
of the upper classes, but they read the Bible instead.
Thus the history and literature of Graeco-Roman and
of the ancient Hebrew civilization were the daily food
of the English mind." If this is to be continued intelligent people who have not the equipment or time for
critical studies must be invited to share in the best that
a reasonable, reverent scholarship can offer.

My thanks are due to Rev. W. T. McCree, M.A.,

[1] Drinkwater: *Outline of Literature,* I, 115.
[2] Cambridge, October 26, 1927.

Streetsville, Ontario, for assistance in reading the proofs; to Chas. Scribner's Sons, for permission to use the Tayler Lewis translation; and to the publishers for their kind coöperation in getting this book into its final form.

W. G. J.

CONTENTS

THE BOOK OF JOB:
ITS SUBSTANCE AND SPIRIT

THE BOOK OF JOB:
ITS SUBSTANCE AND SPIRIT

I

INTRODUCTION

GENERAL CONSIDERATIONS

1. *The English Versions*

Before coming to the specific subject, it may be well to consider the composition, transmission and translation of the ancient books that form our Old Testament. The version that is still in common use was published in 1611; the scholars of that day, when their work was finished, said, "And now at last, by the mercy of God, and the continuance of our labours, it being brought into such a conclusion, as that we have great hopes that the Church of England may reap good fruit thereby." That wish has been abundantly fulfilled, not only England and its churches but the whole English speaking world has reaped "good fruit." It has been called "the worst printed book in the world"; and certainly many improvements can be made in the arrangement of the material. Severe criticism has been spent upon the division into chapters and verses. As to translation it is quite reasonable to expect that, in the course of three centuries, much light should be thrown upon the literary forms and the meaning of particular words. In spite of all its limitations the version of 1611 is not likely to lose its pre-eminence. This is not due to mere tradition or stolid conservatism. The real beauty of the translation has been the cause of its survival and its great influence.

Whatever may be its fortune in the distant future, it was a case of the survival of the fittest. It was the climax of a great movement which could only become widespread after a reading public was made possible by the use of printing. The first English book was printed somewhere about 1474. Wycliffe's translation was about a century earlier. The work of Tyndale and Coverdale in the following century was more important and has had a lasting influence. The subject of translation is a large one; it has had a long history down to our own time. This tribute of the English Revisers to the version that they were asked to correct, and if possible improve, is worth noting: "We have had to study this great Version carefully and minutely, line by line; and the longer we have been engaged upon it the more we have learned to admire its simplicity, its dignity, its power, its happy turns of expression, its general accuracy and we must not fail to add, the music of its cadences and the felicities of its rhythm." The Revised Version of the Old Testament, 1884, has rendered good service and the English reader will find in it much help in various parts of the Book of Job. It has been criticized for making too many changes and also for making too few. It is a good exercise for the student of the English language to note the changes and to compare them with the suggestions of the American Revisers, recorded at the end.

Pages could be filled with tributes by competent authorities on the beauty of the older version and also on the influence it has exerted on English literature and speech. Whatever improvements may be desirable any one who has studied the Hebrew text can bear witness to the courage, reverence, and skill of those who gave us our English Bible. It was made at a flowering period of our language, and where the text is good it is marked by a union of simplicity and beauty, free from the extravagance and affectation which marred so much of the literature of that age. Take for example the beautiful story of the child Samuel (I Sam. III) and note how little the Revisers could find that needed change. In the one verse, thirteen, where there is real difficulty the margin gives us the Greek text which is probably nearest to the original. The same may be said of the picturesque narrative Job I and II. In the case of that noble poem Psalm CVII the situation is similar. Very few changes have been made, some may even question whether much is gained by changing "enemy" to "adversary," "solitary way" to "desert way," but surely "into the haven where they would be" is not as poetic as "unto their desired haven"; fortunately the margin of the Revised Version preserves for us the Hebrew idiom "the haven of their desire." They might have indicated by a space after verse 31 that the remaining twelve verses are probably a separate poem, and have called attention by different type to the refrain: verses 8, 15, 21, 31.

Oh that men would praise Yahweh for His goodness,
And for His wonderful works to the children of men.

On the same principle Psalms XLII, XLIII would have been joined together and the refrain made clear by different type, but the time had not come for that kind of revision and once begun it would have been difficult to know where to stop. The Revised Version, at any rate, did remind people that our Bible did not drop down from heaven in its present form but was a trans-

lation of ancient documents which still need to be
studied in their original form. For students the work
of a host of private translators and commentators are
available.

2. *The Nature and the Need of Criticism*

In this case "criticism" is just another name for the
study which is necessary to the full appreciation of any
great literature, especially in the case of documents
whose origin is far removed from our own time. The
Hebrew (Canonical) literature with which we are concerned took its rise in a period the end of which is more
than two thousand years distant. That so much of it
has been preserved, even if parts of it are in an imperfect condition, is a wonderful thing. It was not graven
on the solid rock but written on perishable material
liable to partial damage that was difficult to repair.
Criticism, in this sense, is simply careful reading by
means of such help as is within our reach. Any one
who notes that in the difficult passage Job xix. 25, 26,
six words are printed in *italics* and that this means not,
as in our usage, emphasis, but the supplying of words
not in the original, is to that extent a critic. Two
thoughts would be suggested by this observation, first
that the text in the original is not clear, and second,
that, in such a case, translation has merged into interpretation. Or to observe the two forms applied to the
God of the Hebrews in our version, "LORD" and
"Lord," and to be led to enquire as to the origin and
meaning of this distinction is to begin a kind of inves-
tigation that may be extended indefinitely in the study
of the text. We may find that in pursuing enquiries
that are often called "pedantic" we are coming into
close contact with the thoughts of men who were anx-

ious to preserve these great spiritual treasures. They were thinking only of their faith and their religious needs, but a larger destiny than they ever dreamed of was appointed for the words of prophets and poets; and so it has come to pass that the scholars who consecrate their learning and skill to the study of ancient texts render a real service to us.

The two aspects of this study are named Textual or Lower Criticism and Literary or Higher Criticism; the first limits itself, as far as possible, to the search after the correct form of the original text; the second is concerned with the larger questions of the nature, structure and significance of a particular book, its place in the literature and life of the nation. The first form of study to be pursued vigorously after the Reformation was the study of the text; at first it met with criticism arising from the belief that the sacred text was perfect and should not be subjected to the tests applied to secular authors. It is now well established and has rendered great service. The careful comparison of manuscripts and Versions belongs to this department but a strict limitation in methods and material is not possible. The latest suggestion in this department is that observation of the poetic form or "metre" can be used in correcting the text. The phrase "Higher Criticism" can be traced back one hundred and fifty years. It was then applied to the analysis of the Pentateuch and declared to be "unknown to no humanist." A general distinction may be made, but naturally these two lines of criticism run into one another, because when the questions are asked about particular additions to the text facts must be considered that pass beyond the mere examination of words. We may take two examples in Micah 1.

For the transgression of Jacob is all this,
And for the sins of the house of Israel.
What is the transgression of Jacob? is it not Samaria?
And what are the high places of Judah, are they not Jeru-
   salem?

Note that in verse 5a we have "transgression" and
"sin" (R. V.) balancing one another, according to the
structure of Hebrew poetry. But in clause 5 we have
"transgression" and "high places"; there the parallelism is lost. The sense is that Micah, the peasant
prophet, whose home is in the country, and whose sym-
pathies are with the poor, denounces Samaria and Jerusalem as the centres of the nation's corruption. The
word "sin" is surely demanded in the second case also.
When we turn to the Greek text we find the word
"sin"; so that the word needed is supplied by the only
other manuscript that goes back to pre-Christian times.
When these two arguments are re-enforced by the
statement that the polemic against "high places" belongs to a later time and that there is no force in
denouncing Jerusalem as a "high place," as it was a
legitimate sanctuary, we are passing a little beyond
mere textual criticism, but the evidence is strengthened.
So we read,

What is the transgression of Jacob? is it not Samaria?
What is the sin of Judah? is it not Jerusalem?

Such cases might be multiplied; another example is
Isaiah vi. 13, where the phrase "the holy seed is the
stock thereof" is regarded as a later addition. The
fact that it is lacking in the Greek, though not in
itself decisive, is important for the textual critics. The
other considerations that it falls out of the metrical
scheme of the chapter, and contains a late phrase "the

holy seed" will have weight varying according to the attitude of the critic to these arguments. Without traversing the whole book we shall find plenty of scope in applying these principles to the poetry of Job.

3. The Conditions That Compel Us to Face These Problems

(a) *Early Bookmaking Composite*. It is important to realise clearly the great difference between the process of book-making in our own and ancient times. We have to face the fact that nearly all the books of the Old Testament are composite, that there are very few that come to us exactly as they left the hand of the original author or compiler. One of the greatest achievements of the last century, however much difference there may be as to details, was to place on a firm footing the belief that the Pentateuch consists of different documents that can be related to various periods in the nation's life. On a much smaller scale we have to apply the same principle to the Book of Job.

(b) *The Hebrew Language*. We shall attempt to show that simple Hebrew narrative and poetry go well into our Anglo-Saxon speech. There is, in fact, a real affinity between the two languages in the lack of inflexions and complicated constructions. But there are disadvantages in the somewhat undeveloped condition of Hebrew. It was essentially a spoken language and much, no doubt, depended on accent and tone. An ancient manuscript is quite unlike a modern printed book. The Hebrew had not a complete vowel system; to make up for the lack of this and to preserve the traditional pronunciation a system of marks, outside of the word, were invented. But these did not come into use until centuries after the language of the Old

Testament had ceased to be a living tongue. All our devices of clearly dividing words and sentences from each other, marking quotations and so forth, are lacking in the unpointed texts. That the manuscripts were copied so carefully and preserved so well is a matter for wonder and admiration. In Isaiah XL. 6, we read, "The voice of one saying Cry, and one said, What shall I cry?" (R. V.) The margin informs the reader that the Greek and Latin translations have "I said" instead of "one said." The sense of the passage is clearly that of these versions as the prophet is speaking of the commission that he received from the heavenly voice. Here is one of the many cases where pronunciation is interpretation. That is a case where the word as it stood there two thousand years ago could be translated in either of these two ways, according as the first syllable was pronounced with the sound of "o" or "a" (ah). In Micah II. 12 there is a case, which cannot be shown without the Hebrew forms, that has caused comment by breaking an important rule of grammar; but, unless any one holds to the infallibility of the Hebrew text, the problem is easily solved by removing the last letter of one word to the beginning of the next. This type can be illustrated only by use of the Hebrew text. Some cases can be explained by remembering that scribes in those days could make the mistakes that come naturally to us in copying or writing from dictation. In Isaiah IX. 3, "Thou hast multiplied the nation *and* not increased the joy." (A. V.) This arrests our attention because we are accustomed to associate growth of population with prosperity. It looks as if the mistake was made by the fact that the word for "not" and for "his" or "its" had the same sound, so we read with R. V., "Thou hast multiplied the nation; thou hast increased their joy." In A. V. Isaiah xl. 3, we read, "The voice of him that crieth in the wilderness, Prepare ye," etc. Here the Greek and Latin agree, but the context makes it clear that we should read with R. V. "The voice of one that crieth, Prepare ye in the wilderness," etc. It is simply a question of the proper division of the clauses of the sentence. After we have made the correction for purposes of exposition, we shall still be haunted by this suggestive phrase in its reference to John the Baptist and others, "a voice crying in the wilderness" (*vox clamantis in deserto*).

(c) *The Way in Which the Text Was Treated Before It Was Regarded as Part of a Sacred Canon.* The evidence points to the conclusion that until quite late in the pre-Christian period there was much freedom in handling the text. The first five books attributed by late tradition to Moses were the first to assume a definite sacred, i.e. a fixed "canonical," character. To-day, with our abundant supply of writing materials, it may seem strange that space in a roll should be so valuable and that some short poems have been rescued from oblivion by finding a corner in some large book with which they had no original connection. Such a case may be the noble poem which found a refuge in two places (Isa. ii. 2-4; Mic. iv. 1-3). Many were no doubt lost, but we are too thankful for what remains to object to the method of their preservation. If any one writes on the margin of a printed book there is no danger of its being confounded with the text; but in the days when the copying was done by hand, the next scribe might easily place such a note in the body of the text, or a verse that had been left out by mistake and then placed in the margin might easily, at the next transcription, be put in the wrong place. Isaiah xl. 5,

a bit of prose in the midst of a poem, seems to be such a
note: "For the glory of Yahweh shall be revealed, and
all flesh shall see it together; for the mouth of Yahweh
hath spoken it." Several scholars so regard Job
XXIII. 8, 9:

Lo to the East I go; He is not there;
Toward the West but I perceive Him not.
To His wondrous works in the North, I look, but look in
    vain;
In the void South He hides Himself, where nought can I
    behold.   (T. L.)

It appears to break the connection though some have
found in it the great thought that it is vain to seek for
God elsewhere than in the human spirit. In some of
these cases we have practical certainty, in others there
is room for difference of opinion.

This kind of criticism is often regarded as "destructive," but if we take an extreme case, in which within
eleven verses ten changes have been made at the suggestion of careful scholars, we may see from the following example that the result increases the clearness and
beauty of the poems.

Isaiah XL.
1. Comfort ye, comfort ye, my people
    Saith your God.
2. Speak ye comfortably unto Jerusalem,
    And say unto her,
That her warfare is accomplished,
    Her iniquity pardoned,
That she hath received from Yahweh's hand double,
    For all her sins.
3. Hark a voice cries prepare in the wilderness,
    The way of Yahweh
Make straight in the desert,
    A highway for our God.

4. Every mountain and hill shall be made low,
   And every valley shall be exalted.
9. Get thee up into the high mountain
   Zion's bringer of good tidings
   Lift up thy voice with strength
   Jerusalem's bringer of good tidings
   Lift it up, be not afraid,
   Proclaim peace
   Say unto the cities of Judah,
   Behold your God
10. Behold the Lord shall come with strength,
    His arm ruling for Him
    Behold His reward is with Him
    And His recompense before Him.
11. He shall feed His flock like a shepherd,
    Gather them with his arm,
    Carry the lambs in His bosom,
    Gently leading the nursing mothers.

———

6. A voice said cry!
   And I said what shall I cry?
   All flesh is grass,
   All its beauty as the flower of the field.
7. The grass withereth, the flower fadeth,
   Because the breath of Yahweh bloweth upon it.
8. The grass withereth, the flower fadeth,
   But the word of our God shall stand for ever.

Note how this short poem breaks the connection of
the two parts of the first and shows a different metre,
equal lines instead of the long and short lines.

(d) *Problems of Translation.* The most difficult
problem is where the text is in poor condition owing
to injury received from wear and tear of the material.
Job xxxix. 13 is given in this form by The International Critical Commentary:

> Is the wing of the ostrich . . .
> Or . . . .

with the statement, "Schultens was already able to collect twenty different translations or interpretations of this verse, and this number could now be considerably increased." A translation for the public could not leave the text in this form; some attempt must be made to discover the sense.

> The wing of the ostrich rejoiceth
> But are her pinions and feathers kindly? (R. V.)

with a marginal note on the last word, "or like the stork's." This passage on "the stupid ostrich" is not important and is possibly a later addition, but it has been a puzzle to translators. The French, following the Latin, does not give much help. "The plumage of the ostrich is like that of the stork and the hawk." One of the curiosities of this kind shows what trouble a word may cause even when the meaning is quite clear. In the same chapter, xxxix. 5:

> Who hath sent out the wild ass?
> Or who hath loosed the bands of the wild ass? (R. V.)

Now it happens that the poet, for the sake of variety, chose an Aramaic word for the end of the second line having the same meaning as the Hebrew word at the end of the first. The versions were content to let the strange word go and to translate "who hath set free the wild ass, and who hath loosed his bands." But the moderns have been so anxious to avoid repetition that in the last line they have resorted to a variety of renderings, such as the zebra, the brayer, the unbridled, the mustang. This kind of research if pursued in detail would lead to "pedantry," so we turn to something more important.

We are sensitive about Psalm xxiii because of its

simple faith and its sacred associations, and it is not likely that, in any case, we shall lose the phrase "the valley of the shadow of death" (*in medio umbrae mortis*), from our literature. But it is worth noting that the large majority of Hebrew scholars have come to the conclusion that Hebrew, unlike Greek and German, except in proper names, does not form compound words. Thus the word, being pronounced differently, means "gloomy" or "deep darkness," without reference to death. It occurs a number of times in Job III. 5; x. 21; XXVIII. 3; XXXIV. 22; XXXVIII. 17. The last passage refers to the lower regions and "gates of darkness" is more suitable than "the gates of the shadow of death." The R. V. retains the usual rendering, giving in the first case "or deep darkness," in the margin.

Another phrase that we would not care to sacrifice at the shrine of grammatical accuracy is "the King of Glory" (Ps. XXIV. 5). It can and has been translated "glorious King" and that is what it means but "King of Glory" has a rich full sound and has sung itself into our hearts. Hebrew because it has few adjectives is compelled to use this form, linking together two nouns one of which expresses the quality of the other. "A man of valour," "a virtuous woman," etc. "The sons of Belial" (I Sam. x. 27) we could well spare and it is a pity that R. V. did not put "base fellows" or "worthless men" into the text instead of leaving it in the margin.

The Sacred Name. One of the most difficult questions that faces the translators is the treatment of the personal name of Israel's God. We have to note here the influence of a long history which cannot be ignored and that we must try to understand. In the early days the Hebrews could use this name with rev-

erent familiarity, as a fierce battle cry: "A sword for
Yahweh and for Gideon" (Judg. VII. 20), or in a gentle
prayer, "Yahweh deal kindly with you, as ye have dealt
with the dead (Ruth I. 8)." But some time before the
Christian era, under a growing sense of the greatness
of their God, and a severe interpretation of certain
passages (Ex. XX. 7; Lev. XIX. 12) the Jewish scribes
began to substitute in the reading of the Old Testament the word "Lord." It was not possible to change
the text, but they indicated that the name was to be
pronounced as if it were "Lord." The combination of
the vowels of the word "lord" in connection with consonants of Yahweh has resulted in the form JEHOVAH
in a few places of the English version (Isa. XII. 2; Ps.
LXXXIII. 18). But the Jewish custom influenced the
early versions, the Greek used *kurios* (lord), the Latin
Dominus, and the English LORD to represent the
Hebrew name Yahweh. The Revisers made very little
change; they tell us that they used Jehovah "in a few
passages in which the introduction of a proper name
seemed to be required." If this principle is once admitted it is difficult to see how it can be confined to "a
few places." Take the question, "How shall we sing
the LORD'S song in a strange land (Ps. CXXXVII. 4)?"
Here the thought is not of the Lord of the world, but
of the national God of Israel worshipped in Jerusalem.
The American Revisers passed this resolution, "Substitute the Divine name Jehovah whenever it occurs
in the Hebrew text for the LORD." The trouble with
"Jehovah" is that it is not a real word but an artificial
form, its hybrid origin clings to it and lends to it an
air of unreality. The name "Yahweh" is no doubt
nearer to the original form but we are told that it is
"too foreign to be domesticated in the English lan-

guage." "The Eternal" has been tried but it is neither correct nor suitable, and in many passages its effect is grotesque. "An American Translation" (1927) goes back to the English usage and asks its readers to remember that behind the word LORD there is the Hebrew name Yahweh.

The word "Torah" is one that should not always be represented by the same word in English. A great word that lives long must pass through varied shades of meaning. Here also we have an interesting history; to the Jew this word came finally to mean the Pentateuch or Law of Moses. Long before that it meant "to teach" then the result of such teaching in a precept or precepts; in Isaiah i. 10; ii. 3; the marginal readings of R. V., "teaching" and "instruction," are suitable, while in Psalms i, xix and cxix "law" expresses the idea, as there is probably a reference to a body of written laws that can be made the subject of study.

The name "Sheol" is making a brave attempt to secure for itself a place in Biblical literature, but the English reader does not feel that it is quite at home.

> Where groan the giant shades
> Whose dwelling is beneath the waters
> All bare before Him Sheol lies
> And deep Abaddon [1] hath no covering.
>
> (Job xxvi. 5, 6, T. L.)

Here Sheol is evidently "The Underworld." The American Revisers made a clean sweep with the instruction to "substitute 'Sheol' where it occurs in the Hebrew text for the rendering 'the grave,' 'the pit,' and 'hell' and omit these renderings from the margin." The English Revisers have left the different translations in the historical passages and kept Sheol for the margin

[1] Destruction, personified.

there, but in the poetical sections they have placed the
Hebrew word in the text. The reason given is that
"hell" has lost its primitive meaning and now has the
sense of a separate place of torment. But from one
magnificent poem they felt that "hell" could not be dis-
lodged as it is used in more of its original sense and is
less liable to be misunderstood. A part of this passage
(Isa. XIV. 9-15) may be quoted for comparison with the
poetry of Job:

> Hell from beneath is moved for thee,
>   To meet thee at thy coming,
> It stirreth up the dead for thee,
>   All the Kings of the earth;
> And they shall speak
>   And say unto thee,
> Art thou become weak as we?
>   Art thou become like unto us?
> Thy pomp is brought down to the ground,
>   And the noise of thy viols.
> The worm is spread under thee,
>   And the worms cover thee.
> How art thou fallen from heaven!
>   O Lucifer son of the morning.
> How art cast down to the ground!
>   Which didst weaken the nations.
> For thou hast said in thine heart,
>   I will ascend into heaven,
> I will exalt my throne
>   Above the stars of God.
> I will sit upon the Mount of the Congregation,
>   In the sides of the North.
> I will ascend upon the heights of the clouds,
>   I will be like the Most High.
> Yet thou shalt be brought down to hell.   (R. V.)

This passage is a tremendously powerful picture of
the divine vengeance on a cruel, arrogant tyrant. The

word "hell," with its terrible associations, helps to strengthen the impression of relentless doom. The commotion in the underworld at the coming of the august victim, this new addition to the company of the damned, the grim greeting from the ghostly forms, with its reminder that here all share the same corruption—every stroke increases the powerful impression of this awful picture. This is surely right, that in translating an important word it is necessary to enter into the feeling of the passage. To the Hebrews death, the grave, and the dim, dismal world of the dead were closely connected; thought might linger sadly on any particular phase of that which must be the end of each man's earthly life. "Sheol," however, is likely for long to have a foreign sound to English ears.

Space cannot be devoted here to textual criticism. There is abundance of that in the learned commentaries. When in Job xxxix. 24, in the splendid description of the war-horse we meet the sentence, "Neither believeth he that it is the sound of the trumpet," any careful reader must feel that there is something wrong. We are driven to regard the line as secondary, or to amend by the aid of the Versions. The nearest is "he standeth not still at the sound of the trumpet," or "he is not afraid of the sound of the trumpet," but we hanker after something more positive and lively, as, " 'Tie hard to hold him in when the trumpets sound."

(e) *Hebrew Poetry*. When the great English Version was made there had been no special research into the nature of Hebrew poetry, and no attempt was made to distinguish, by the form of printing, between poetry and prose. The Revisers changed this in the strictly poetical books, Job, Psalms, Proverbs, and Song of

Songs, but not in the Prophets. Still the translators
of the A. V. have done so well that we know that they
must have felt the poetic power that comes to us
through their work. The formal arrangement helps us
but there are many passages where the prose form cannot hide the real poetry.

> Lift up your heads, O ye gates,
> And be ye lift up, ye everlasting doors,
> And the King of Glory shall come in.
> Who is this King of Glory?
> Yahweh strong and mighty,
> Yahweh mighty in battle.   (Ps. xxiv.)

> But the redeemed shall walk there,
> And the ransomed of Yahweh shall return
> And come with singing unto Zion;
> And everlasting joy shall be upon their heads;
> They shall obtain joy and gladness,
> And sorrow and sighing shall flee away.
>   (Isa. xxxv. 10.)

> Arise shine; for thy light is come,
> And the glory of Yahweh is risen upon thee.
> For behold darkness shall cover the earth,
> And gross darkness the peoples;
> But Yahweh shall rise upon thee,
> And His glory shall be seen upon thee.
>   (Isa. lx. 1, 2.)

These, when properly read, produce the effect of noble
poetry in whatever form they may be printed; they
show that Hebrew poetry in its simplicity and strength
can be represented in our own language and that the
men who did this work in the sixteenth and seventeenth
centuries got very near to the heart of their originals.

The following passage keeps fairly close to the sense,
as may be seen by comparison with our versions, and
there is certainly a suggestion of rhythm.

It is as I have seen, that they who evil plough,
Who mischief sow, they ever reap the same.
By the breath of God these perish utterly;
By the blast of His fierce wrath are they consumed.
(Hushed is) the lion's cry, the jackal's roar;
The strong young lion's teeth are crushed.
The fierce old lion perishes from want;
The lion's whelps are scattered far and wide;

(Job iv. 8-11, J. L.)

Even if this is a later expansion of the couplet that
the poet puts into the mouth of Eliphaz:

Call now to mind; when has the guiltless perished?
And where were just men hopelessly destroyed? (IV. 7.)

it shows that something of his spirit and style was
caught by early students of the book.

When the temple was destroyed it seems that the
tradition as to metre, musical terms, etc., was practically lost and in later times the MSS. were, in this
respect, carelessly copied and the poetical form preserved in only a few cases or in the best MSS. Bishop
R. Lowth published in 1753 his "Lectures on the Sacred
Poetry of the Hebrews" (*"Praelectiones de Sacra Poesi
Hebraeorum"*). Since then the principle of parallelism
has been clearly recognised, though his work, at first,
had more influence on German than on English scholars. He said:

This much, I think we may be allowed to infer from the
alphabetic poems, viz. that the Hebrew poems are written
in verse, properly so-called, that the harmony of the verses
does not arise from rhyme, that is from similar corresponding sounds terminating the verses, but from some sort of
rhythm, probably some sort of metre, the laws of which are
unknown, wholly undiscoverable.

Since that time much energy and skill have been spent
on the subject of "metre," the result may seem to be

small, but the principle of parallelism has been clearly recognised and abundantly illustrated. Reuss puts it strongly, "Parallelism, or the regular placing side by side of symmetrically constructed clauses is not so much a feature of Hebrew poetry as its very nature." Other scholars have discovered variations that we are tempted to call "fancy forms" but they appear to be simply developments of the three to which attention was called by Lowth.

(1) Synonymous, when the original thought is repeated or echoed in different but equivalent terms.

> Lo! He goes by me but I see Him not;
> Sweeps past, but I perceive Him not.   (Job. ix. 11.)

> How brief the triumph of the bad!
> The joy of the impure how momentary!
>
> (Job xx. 5.)

(2) The Antithetic. The second line expresses a clear contrast to the first. A favourite form in proverbial literature. (Cf. Prov. xii.)

> A wise son maketh a glad father:
> But a foolish son is the heaviness of his mother.
>
> (Prov. x. 1.)

(3) The Synthetic. The thought is expanded in the second line.

> Our fathers have sinned and are not,
> And we have borne their iniquities.   (Lam. v. 7.)

> O now make friends with Him, and be at peace,
> For in so doing good shall come to thee.
>
> (Job. xxii. 21.)

As there is so much sustained speech in the book of Job, there is a tendency to the prevalence of this form. At this point, before considering the question of metre, the following statement by B. Duhm, as a brief appre-

ciation, may be useful. Speaking of the poet of Job
he says:

He has written his poem with his heart's blood, and certainly more for himself than for the great public. His own
feelings, doubts, demands, and hopes he places in the mouth
of Job. Only the speeches of God *must* give the conclusion
and final consolation. The three friends have to represent
the view of their own and of an earlier time, with which
the poet is not satisfied; in their speeches the Deuteronomic
theory of retribution, with its modifications finds expression.
Concerning the eschatological expectations, which created
excitement in his time, the poet has no word to say. As to
poetic form he chooses the simplest metre of Hebrew pros-
ody, the verse of four lines, each with three accents. His
poetry has not the tremendous weight of the speeches of
Amos, the majestic power of Isaiah's discourses, the spirit-
stirring movement of Hosea's quatrains, the spiritual charm
of Jeremiah' lyrics, nor the enthusiastic pathos of Deutero-
Isaiah; corresponding to the post-classical period and the
greater age of the poet, he is not always free from a certain diffuseness and a cumbrous fluency, but he reflects the
bold spirit, the dramatic energy, the creative imagination
of a great poet and finds, at the right time, the most effective expressions for the fierce struggles of a spirit, which
knows itself quite alone, and contends almost alone for
man's highest good, the faith that there is righteousness in
the world.

When it comes to disputed questions about "metre,"
they cannot be very well discussed apart from the
Hebrew text; this fact almost limits us to the points
where there is general agreement. This parallelism
or balancing of expressions was not invented by the
Hebrews. It is found in earlier literatures and goes
back to the natural impulse towards rhythmical movement; but in their poets and prophets it finds its most
perfect and powerful expression.

The line is the metrical unit and the couplet the
commonest form; the divisions in the sense coincide

with the end of the line. This means the absence of "run-on" lines, so that we look in vain for passages of the same structure as the following where we have seven lines without a stop at the end of the line:

> Sing, Heavenly Muse, that on the secret top
> Of Oreb, or of Sinai didst inspire
> That shepherd who first taught the chosen seed
> In the beginning how the heavens and earth
> Rose out of Chaos; or if Zion hill
> Delight thee more, and Siloa's brook that flowed
> Fast by the oracle of God, I thence
> Invoke thy aid to my adventurous song.

Traces of rhyme have been found, whether accidental or designed, but, while the story-tellers and poets found significance in similarity of sounds, rhyme is not really a feature of Hebrew verse. Rhymed translations of the Psalms, in many forms, have been used in Church services, but the rhythmical form suitable for intoning or chanting is probably nearer to the usage of temple and synagogue.

There is rhythm, for without that it would not be poetry; it is produced by a regular succession of beats or accents. The commonest form is that of two or four equal lines of three accents to each line and this is the prevailing form in the Book of Job.

> O blessed is the man whom God reproves;
> The Almighty's chastening therefore spurn thou not.
>
> (v. 17.)

That the original work of the poet was cast in units of four lines is a drastic theory demanding too much uniformity on the part of a great artist.[2] This rules out XIX. 12:

[2] The result of Bickel's theory combined with a particular view as to the value of the Greek text may be seen in Dr. Dillon's "The Sceptics of the Old Testament," where the poem is reduced to 309 verses of four lines each. See the *International Critical Commentary.*

> Together draw His troops;
>   At me cast up their way;
> Around my tent they come

and similar passages. In the Greek this verse has only
two lines and there are other considerations, but scholars generally do not admit that metrical variation *alone*
can decide the genuineness or otherwise of a passage.
Each case must be considered on its merits.

In this connection it is not necessary to do more than
notice the so-called "kinah-strophe" or elegiac measure,
the line with three beats followed by two:

> She is fallen to rise no more,
>   The Virgin of Israel
> Spread out upon her land,
>   None to upraise her.   (Amos v. 2.)

> How doth she sit all alone
>   The (once) populous city!
> How hath she come to be widowed
>   Once great among nations?

> She that was queen among kingdoms
>   Now come under tribute!
> She bitterly weeps in the night
>   With her tears on her cheek.

> She hath not a one to bring comfort
>   Out of all her lovers
> Her friends are turned traitors towards her
>   They have come to be enemies.[3]

While highly suitable for this class of poems this
measure is not confined to it.[4]

The question of strophes in the larger sense is easily
settled where there is a mechanical arrangement such
as Psalm cxix, where we find eight lines beginning
with "a," eight with "b," and so on through the alpha-

---

[3] See E. G. King, *Early Religious Poetry of the Hebrews* (Cambridge), p. 154, for list of books on this subject.

[4] See Ps. xix, 7ff., and the passage from Isaiah previously
quoted.

bet; or where the poem is divided into sections by a refrain, e.g. Psalms XLII, XLIII, one poem with the verse, "Why art thou cast down O my soul," etc., repeated three times. Psalm XLVI. 6, 7, "Yahweh of Hosts is with us; the God of Jacob is our refuge"; it has probably dropped out after v. 3; Isaiah IX. 12, 17, 21; x. 4, "For all this His anger is not turned away, but His hand is stretched out still." There is nothing like this in the Book of Job, except XXVIII. 12, 20, "But where shall wisdom be found? And where is the place of understanding?" This refrain also may have accidentally dropped out in other parts of that poem which probably does not belong to the original part of the book. Two of the "stanzas" used by Dillon may be quoted and for purpose of comparison, followed by another private translation.

CLXX

Lo, I cry out against violence, but I am not heard;
I cry aloud but there is no judgment.
He hath fenced up my way that I cannot pass;
He has set darkness in my paths.

CLXXI

He hath stripped me of my glory,
And taken the crown from my head.
On all sides hath he ruined me, and I am undone;
And mine hope hath he felled like a tree.

. . . .

Behold I cry of wrong but am not heard;
I cry aloud but there is no redress.
For He hath fenced my road; I cannot pass;
And darkness hath He set o'er all my ways,
My glory from me hath He stripped,
And from my head the crown removed.
On all sides doth He crush me; I am gone;
And like a tree uproots He all my hope.

(xix. 7-10, T. L.)

II

THE BOOK OF JOB

1. Unsolved Problems

(a) *Form of the Poetry.* This question of the precise form of the poetry does not seem to admit of the rigid definition attempted by some scholars, neither is such precision necessary to the understanding and appreciation of the poems. It is clear that rhythmical couplets of the evenly balanced kind which we have found elsewhere are the prevailing form, and that in the original each of the two lines has three accents or stresses. Further in these connected speeches it is not surprising that in arranging the aspects of the thought that verses, in our sense of the word, can be discovered consisting of four lines:

> And now my very life is poured out;
> The days of my affliction hold me fast
> By night my every bone is pierced above;
> My throbbing nerves (within me) never sleep.
> (xxx. 16, 17.)

The reference to "night" and "day" gives a kind of unity to these four lines; and so links the couplets together.

> Behold all this mine eye hath seen;
> Mine ear hath heard and understood it well.
> What ye know I do also know;
> In nothing do I fall below you.   (xiii. 1, 2.)

Should we follow Duhm and Dillon, putting xiv. 13
thus:

O that thou wouldest hide me in Sheol!
That thou wouldest secret me till thy wrath be past.
That thou wouldest appoint me a set time and remember me!
If so be man could die and yet live on!

or treat the first three lines as a separate verse, as is
generally done, and render the fourth line, "If a man
die will he live (again)"? This type of problem is in
many cases not simple, because the question of metre
is difficult to disentangle from other elements. This
example may be sufficient to show the kind of problem
that the conscientious commentator must face. But
it must be dismissed here with the statement that the
concensus of opinion among scholars is that these
investigations into metrical forms are helpful in the
study of the text, but are rarely sufficient when taken
alone to settle a crucial point. We may be told, on
one side, that Oriental poets had "symmetrio-phobia"
or an intense dislike of being bound too tightly by
conventional bonds, and on the other, that having once
chosen a particular form for a certain piece of work
they kept rigidly to it. Perhaps here there is safety
in the middle course.

(b) *Relations of the Hebrew and Greek Texts.*
Another of these practically insoluble problems, which,
while it may influence our choice of selections, cannot
be discussed in detail, is the relations of the Greek
and Hebrew texts with their complicated histories. In
view of our present purpose, it is an interesting suggestion that even in those early days "an abbreviator
was at work." The fact that "the defect is not at all
evenly distributed over the book inclines the balance

against the priority of the Greek; it would have been natural for an abbreviator to shorten increasingly in the successive cycles, which in general cover much the same ground, and most of all in the speeches of Elihu which contribute so little that is fresh." In one of the smaller commentaries [1] we find an interesting, careful discussion, and, as a result of the work of many specialists, we have the statement that, apart from longer sections which must be considered on their merits,

a careful study of the subject indicates that the translator was wont to omit what appeared to him to be repetitions in altered forms. Sometimes this led him to omit a mere phrase; sometimes, the second member of a parallelism; sometims a verse or more which for emphasis restates the thought in altered form; sometimes quotations from other parts of the poem; and sometimes, difficult passages. When once this tendency on the part of the translator is recognised, the necessity of regarding with suspicion every line or verse that this translation omits is removed.

Only those, however, who have made an effort to read the texts and compare the versions can form an adequate idea of the difficulty and complexity of the subject.

The following words of XLII. 17 added in Greek and other versions are: "But it is written that he shall be raised with those whom the Lord shall raise up" [2] and

---

[1] Dr. G. A. Barton, Macmillan, 1911.

[2] It is interesting to note this view of the reward of the godly man in a metrical version of Psalm XCI by J. Montgomery (1771-1854).

> Here for grief reward thee double,
> Crown with life beyond the grave,

where the original is,

> With long life will I satisfy him
> And show him my salvation.

the words put into the mouth of Job's wife, II. 9 "How
long wilt thou be steadfast, saying Behold, I will wait
a little time expecting the hope of my salvation? For
behold thy memorial has perished from the earth, thy
sons and daughters, the labours and pangs of my womb,
whom in vain I bore with pains. Thou sitting in the
corruption of worms, passing the night in the open
air, while I, even as a hired slave, wander from place
to place, and from house to house, longing for the
setting of the sun, that I may rest from the hardships
and toils that encompass me" are certainly not translations from the Hebrew original where the story is
marked by a picturesque brevity. Later legend
delighted in such expansions.

(c) *An Intricate Question*. 1. Another riddle has
come to us owing to the form in which the speeches of
the friends have been preserved. The book, as it
stands, consists of:

I The Narrative Portions, Chapters I, II, XLII. 7-17
II The speeches of Job and the Friends, chapters
III-XXXI
III The speeches of Elihu, Chapters XXXII-XXXVII
IV The speeches of the Almighty and Job's brief
replies, chapters XXXVIII-XLII. 6.

It is generally accepted that there are sections large
or small that do not belong to the book in its earliest
form, some of these will call for careful consideration;
but a peculiar problem arises in connection with the
chapters XXV-XXVII, in what should be the concluding
series of speeches by the friends. Bildad's speech is
very short, and Zophar does not speak at all. It has
been suggested that in this way the poet indicates that
the friends have exhausted their arguments and begin

at this point to feel that they can no longer stand
against Job's vigorous and persistent defence of his
integrity and his passionate appeals to God. This
would appear in any case to be rather a clumsy dramatic device, but the strongest arguments against it
are that some parts of these speeches do not seem to
be in Job's vein and express opinions which he has
been attacking. This points to a dislocation which
many scholars have recognised, but when attempts are
made to put matters right various solutions are
offered. It looks as if parts of this section had been
lost and that portions only of Bildad's and Zophar's
speeches had survived in a disordered condition. There
are many proposals; their variety seems to show that
the problem is very difficult if not insoluble. We have
to admit that, while the poet is not writing a logical
treatise and is subject to changing moods, in the face
of his difficulties, yet we must allow him a substantial
consistency in regard to the central principles of the
controversy. The following passage ascribed to Job
has the genuine ring.

> As liveth God who turns away my plea,
> The Almighty One who hath distressed my soul,
> So long as breath remains to me,
> And in my nostrils dwell Eloah's life,
> These lips of mine shall never say the wrong,
> My tongue shall never murmur what is false,
> Away the thought, I'll not confess to you;
> Nor mine integrity unto my latest breath renounce,
> My right I hold, I will not let it go;
> My heart shall not reproach me while I live.

(XXVII. 2-6.)

But this is immediately followed by lines that seem
more suitable to Zophar, and are regarded by some as
part of his third and final speech:

Let mine enemy be as the wicked,
And let him that riseth up against me be as the unrighteous
For what is the hope of the godless when God cutteth him
    off,
When God taketh away his soul
Will God hear his cry
When trouble cometh upon him?
Will he delight himself in the Almighty
And call upon God at all times?   (xxvii. 7-10.)

But round these three chapters we move with uncertain steps; we may find a path for ourselves but we cannot be sure that it is the original highway. The exercise is useful for those who have the time and taste, but the great message of the book can be grasped without the settlement of all these problems.

2. *Analysis of the Book*

In addition to what has been said in the previous paragraph regarding the contents of the book and the divisions of its chief parts, questions must be discussed on which, fortunately, there is a large measure of agreement among modern scholars. It does not fall within our plan to discuss in detail the large number of the smaller insertions, though some of them are used incidentally as illustrations. But there are two problems of this kind that must be faced if we are to gain a reasonable view of the Book.

(*a*) *A Specimen of Wisdom Literature* (xxviii). The fact that the Book of Job itself has a place in this class of literature will need fuller consideration, but here we note the fact that anyone reading carefully through the speeches will observe the slight connection, if any, of xxviii with the context. The aversion to "cutting up the book" did for a long period lead to many attempts to make out a real connection.

It might, no doubt, be supposed that Job, no longer irritated by the retorts of his friends, has reached a calmer mood; and abandoning the attempts to discover a *speculative* solution of the perplexities which distress him, finds man's wisdom to consist in the *practical* fulfilment of the duties of life. But a serious difficulty arises in connection with what follows. If Job has risen to this tranquil temper, how comes it that he falls back (xxx. 20-23) into complainings and dissatisfaction at not having been justified by God (xxxi. 35)?[3]

The reader who makes no claim to critical scholarship will probably feel that a separate subject is here treated in a different temper. The linguistic evidences, of which we cannot expect much in one chapter, point in the same direction; the word "Lord" (xxviii) occurs nowhere else in the book, and the Hebrew word behind the word "God" is rarely used in the speeches (v. 8; xx. 29). In verses 12 and 20 there is the refrain, "Where can wisdom be found," etc., and it may have dropped out from other places. This is peculiar and would be more natural in a separate poem.

(*b*) *The Elihu Speeches* (xxxii-xxxvii). This is a more important question, but there is very large agreement among scholars that these chapters are not an original part of the book, that they cannot possibly come from the pen of the great poet who wrote the dialogue. Froude, in his interesting essay on "The Book of Job," based upon three German commentaries, and written over seventy years ago, recognised that the verdict of Hebrew scholars, even then, was against the genuineness of these speeches. The statement can be made more strongly now. The question is important not merely because of the size of this section—about one-fifth of the whole book—but also because of

[3] Driver, I. C. C., p. 233.

its bearing on the interpretation of the poet's attitude towards the central problem of suffering. The critic who thinks that he has shown that "the connection of these speeches with the rest of the book leaves nothing to be desired" has not convinced many competent judges.

Previous naming in the prologue was not practicable, and does not correspond to the poet's custom elsewhere; on the other hand, he has declared by hints sufficiently clear that he thinks of the dialogues as taking place in the presence of an audience (XVII. 9; XVIII. 2; XXX. 1) that has gradually gathered together that might be split into parties on the one side or the other, and from which at any time a speaker might arise. The sentence, XXXI. 40 (The words of Job are ended) instead of being a useless addition is of the highest critical value as a true token; it is the best beginning that one can think of for the introduction of this speaker whose contribution, when the original text is restored, is perfectly suitable and corresponds to the poet's usage elsewhere.[*]

Even such heroic efforts have not been able to stem the tide. This view tends to make the doctrine of the disciplinary view of suffering not merely one of the solutions which emerge in the course of the discussion but the main aim and purpose of the book. That subject will need to be considered in a larger connection. Even on a superficial reading of the book we are arrested by striking differences from anything that we have met: XXXII. 1-5, a long prose introduction of a new speaker. Verse 6, "And Elihu the son of Barachel answered and said"; (XXXIV. 1) "Moreover Elihu answered and said"; (XXXV. 1) the same; (XXXVI. 1) "Then Elihu continued and said." It must be admitted that this continual *answering* when the man has the field all to himself does not seem to be easy to

[*] K. Budde, p. XVIII.

explain. The suggestion that the poet added these
sections later to make his view clearer, but had not
time to polish them and bring them to the same excellence as the other speeches does not make a very strong
appeal. The linguistic side of the argument which has
been examined to the minutest details cannot be discussed here. Dr. Driver who was remarkable for his
careful scholarship and well-balanced judgment says:

> The style is prolix, laboured and somewhat tautologous
> (xxxii. 6, 10b, 17b); the power and brilliancy which are
> so conspicuous in the poem generally are sensibly missing.
> The reader, as he passes from Job and his three friends to
> Elihu, is conscious at once that he has before him the work
> of a writer, not indeed devoid of literary skill, but certainly
> inferior in literary and poetical genius to the rest of the
> book. The language is often involved and the thought
> strained.

Budde concedes this but seeks to break the force of
this argument by finding extensive interpolations,
about thirty verses, and much corruption. This kind
of criticism can be appreciated, to some extent, even
in the English version. But we are dependent on
experts for the judgment that in the original of these
chapters the language is more strongly tinged with
Aramaic and has many peculiarities of vocabulary
and style.

On the following points any intelligent reader can
form an opinion: (1) The absence of Elihu from the
beginning and end of the popular story. If, as has
been suggested, he was brought in later, one would
have expected him to be mentioned at the close when
judgment is given upon the disputants. His complete
absence from the prologue and epilogue is difficult to
account for. (2) These speeches do not contribute

anything to the substance of the book; the idea that
suffering may be a discipline has been expressed in
more graceful forms by the friends. If the Elihu
speeches were taken out they would leave no real gap;
they come in, a disturbing element, between Job's
final appeal (XXXI. 35-37) and the speech of the
Almighty. Thus the artistic unity, power, and progress of the book are seriously marred. (3) A careful
examination and comparison of Elihu's statements
with the parts that go before and come after has produced on the minds of many students the impression
that the man who wrote these speeches had acquired
a familiarity with the original book. They repeat what
has been said and to some extent anticipate what God
is about to say. In the latter case they tend to weaken
what the poet no doubt meant to be the real climax
of the book.

(c) *The Conclusion of the Discussion.* There is a
growing belief among students that after the series
of dialogues the discussion is brought to a close by one
speech of Yahweh's (XXXVIII. 2-XXXIX. 30; XL. 2) and
one confession by Job (XL. 40-XLII. 2-6). To remind
us of the uncertainty of such criticism and warn us
against dogmatism there is the difference of opinion as
to the genuineness of the passage in Yahweh's speech
(XL. 6-14); Verse 6, "Then Yahweh answered Job out
of the storm and said," is repeated from XXXVIII. 1;
verse 7, "Gird up thy loins," etc., is repeated from
XXXVIII. 3. The remainder, 8-14, makes a very interesting and impressive passage.

> Wilt thou annul my right?
> Condemn me that thou mayest be justified?
> Hast thou an arm like God?
> Or canst thou thunder with a voice like Him?

Put on thee now thy glory and thy pride;
With majesty and beauty deck thyself.
Then send abroad thy o'erflowing wrath,
And look on every proud one, bring him low.
Behold the lofty, humble him;
Tread down the wicked in their place,
Together hide them in the dust,—
Their faces in the darkenss bind,
So will I also praise thee,
Thine own right hand can save thee.   (T. L.)

Seeing that XL. 15-XLI. 34, is generally regarded as a later addition, this speech (XL. 8-14) is very short and those who think that it is genuine must attach it to XL. 2 (omitting 1).

Will the reprover contend with the Almighty?
He that argueth with God, let him answer it.

Would the poet have weakened the effect of that direct challenge by adding these few verses whose gist seems to be that a man who through lack of power is utterly unfit to rule the world is not in a position to criticise the actual Ruler? The view set forth that man has not the wisdom to rule the world and would by rash action make things worse if he were in a position to try—that is a doctrine that needs no proof.

There is much greater agreement about the passage XL. 15-XLI. 34, the descriptions of Behemoth and Leviathan, that it comes from a different author, a man of inferior powers, who wished to illustrate the greatness of God, his distance from frail man by elaborate, extravagant pictures of the hippopotamus and the crocodile—two of the most wonderful of His creatures. It is long since this was recognized by men who exercised literary criticism.[5] As may be seen from the specimens given, these descriptions can be turned into pic-

[5] Since Eichhorn 1854, so Budde p. 241.

turesque English and there is a certain childlike wonder that is admirable. It has been pointed out that
in the genuine speech the sense and reality of the
Divine appeal is kept alive by a series of urgent questions (xxxix. 1, 5, 9, 11, 12, etc.) which stand out in
sharp contrast to the minute, long, drawn-out descriptions of these two strange creatures. To raise the question whether this passage is a unity is not in our line;
neither can the question as to the mythological character of these animals be discussed at length. This is
an ancient Jewish interpretation which has been
revived and strongly supported. It is interesting but
has little bearing on the interpretation of the original
book.

Both poems would, on the basis of a quite superficial
view of xl. 8-14, prove the weakness of men and do this
in long bombastic descriptions, which in their exaggerations
do not keep to the truth; the two quatrains of the poet on
the wild ass are worth more than these twenty-one, which
of course, imposed on the later Jews, so that out of these
two beasts of the Nile they made mythical monsters. If
now and then interpreters have followed them in that
respect, that is at least an indirect proof that these poems
do not betray much of the naturalness and sense of reality
that marks the poet of Job! [6]

A keen remark, worthy of its author!

(d) *The Book That Is Left*. These passages may
be capable of a further analysis but unless we follow
the representatives of a more drastic criticism there is
still a fairly large book left; that is true even if a
quarter of it consists of later additions. The book is a
classic; tributes to its greatness have been paid by men
of the highest distinction from Luther to Carlyle.

[6] B. Duhm.

A number of these are given by J. Strahan,[7] concluding with this from Carlyle.

I call it, apart from all theories about it, one of the grandest things ever written with pen. One feels, indeed, as if it were not Hebrew; such a noble universality, different from noble patriotism, or noble sectarians, reigns in it. A noble Book; all men's Book. It is our first, oldest statement of the never-ending Problem,—Man's destiny, and God's way with him here in this earth. And all in such full flowing outlines, grand in its sincerity, in its simplicity, in its epic melody and repose of reconcilement . . . sublime sorrow, sublime reconciliation; oldest choral melody as of the heart of mankind—so soft, and great, as the summer midnight, as the world with its seas and stars. There is nothing written I think, in the Bible or out of it, of equal literary merit.

But it has not been a popular book in the same sense as the Psalter. In reading the New Testament we have abundant evidence that the Psalms appealed to the hearts of the people, nourishing their piety and keeping alive their religious enthusiasm. It has been claimed that there is only one definite quotation from Job in the New Testament; "He taketh the wise in their own craftiness" (v. 13; I Cor. III. 19). Other allusions have been suggested: XXXIX. 30, "And where the slain are there is she" (i.e. the vulture); Matt. XXIV. 28; Luke XVII. 37: XXIII. 19, "And when he hath tried me I shall come forth as gold" (I Peter I. 7). A careful examination might yield more results, but the fact remains that it has not left a deep impression on the popular mind. On the other hand, the facts that we have been considering show that in the inner circle of scribes and scholars it called forth great lit-

[7] P. 28.

erary activity. The work of scholars in the last century and earlier point in the same direction; it is clear
that it has claimed the attention of special students
more than of the general public. Their investigations
of its contents and the relation of its different parts
has borne good fruit. Just as we know more about
Isaiah of Jerusalem when a small part of the book
that bears his name is ascribed to him, than when the
whole sixty-six chapters were claimed for him, so the
recognition of later additions to Job will enable us
to see more clearly the real problem of the book, and
how it was faced by the great poet.

(e) *It Is a Book That Remains.* When it has been
clearly proved that additions have been made to the
original book, there still remains, in the view of the
great majority of scholars a *real book*—that is one with
a plan and purpose. This means that joined to the
popular story furnished by tradition we have a series
of discussions, the speech of the Almighty, and Job's
final confession. We may admit that in addition to
the fact that separate pieces could only stand a chance
of living by finding a home in a large book, there is
the fact also that orthodox Jews would have found
great difficulty in receiving Job and Ecclesiastes into the
Canon unless an attempt was made to tone down what
seemed to them expressions too sceptical or violent for
a sacred book. The question arising out of these con-
cessions is how far these additions and especially the
dislocations are the result of the adventures and accidents to which ancient books were liable, and how
far to deliberate hostility to the free spirit and daring
discussions which give the special character to this
book. On that point there may never be anything like

unanimity.   It is interesting to find a modern Jew
writing the following passage.

Without doubt the book was considered sacrilegious, and
it is not inconceivable, in fact it is easily possible, that the
scroll may have been torn up to be publicly burned, just as
two hundred years previously the prophecies of Jeremiah
were torn up by Jehoiakim before being consigned to the
flames.   And to carry the parallel to the prophet himself,
even as Jeremiah was spirited away by Shaphan and so
saved from the execution of the death-sentence, may not
possibly the Book of Job, by some means, have been saved
from utter destruction by some devoted disciple, who,
though unable to restore the original order, faithfully preserved every fragment of the mutilated copy.   But about
all this we can have no positive knowledge whatever.   The
only point of which we may feel certain is that the book
was contrary to the orthodox spirit of the times—a fact
which makes its acceptance in the Old Testament Canon a
most perplexing problem.   If we had but some record of the
circumstances which brought about the inclusion of the
Book in Sacred Literature, we would be afforded an insight
into the cross-currents of thought and the spiritual life of
these times which is at present denied us.[6]

It has been suggested that the confusion in connection with the third cycle of speeches was the result not
of accident but of deliberate design.

To make the task of converting an unorthodox production into a bulwark of the Faith, it was necessary to attack
the original book as well.   By additions here and there, by
pious comments inserted at appropriate places, by enlarging
upon the counter arguments presented by the three friends
of Job, by giving a turn to some of Job's utterances different from the one that he had in mind, and also by the more
radical procedure of putting utterances into Job's mouth
which would have a meaning only if spoken by one of the

[6] Buttenwieser, p. xi.

friends, since they directly contradict the fundamental position assumed by Job—such means had to be employed in order to give a flavour of orthodoxy *also* to the original book. This flavour while strong enough to satisfy an age not accustomed to too critical a scrutiny, and which still lacked a complete sense of personal authorship in composition, was, however, not strong enough to endure the test of the critical method in the study of the Old Testament, that set in at the close of the eighteenth century and that reached its climax in our own days.[7]

One, while admiring thorough criticism, may doubt whether the Jewish revision was as cunning as all this implies. But we must admit that partly through accident and partly through an attempt to soften the clash between Job's outspoken speeches and the central beliefs of that time the book has been brought into a condition that makes it less easy to grasp clearly its main outlines. So that while it has furnished interesting problems for special students its popular use has been curtailed.

[7] M. Jastrow, Jr., p. 90.

III

THE INTERPRETATION OF THE BOOK

1. *A Real Book Survives the Ordeal, and So Can Be Interpreted as a Whole*

We begin with the conviction that there is a book to interpret, and not a mere patchwork or series of fragments. In a conservative treatment of the subject marked by a fine gift of exposition, Dr. Bradley, then Dean of Westminster, made the following statement which would apply just as well in 1929 as in 1888. Presenting to a popular audience the arguments against the genuineness of the Elihu speeches, he said:

I have not shrunk from putting these arguments plainly before you. No educated person in the present generation can read the book of Job without having to take them into consideration. They stand on a quite different level from the theories of critics who would reject chapter after chapter till they had reduced this great work to a mere unintelligible and formless torso, on which we are to suppose various authors to have built up by degrees the great and noble poem which we are studying. Such theories have in turn their day, and have passed, or are rapidly passing into oblivion. But the position and significance of the next six chapters (*i.e.* the speeches of Elihu) are wholly different and far more perplexing.[1]

We may not be able to stand precisely in the same position as this scholar, and we are compelled to apply to other cases the arguments that he recognises in

[1] *The Book of Job*, p. 288.

the case of Elihu's discourses, but the "vigour and
rigour" of the criticism that reduces the book to a
sceptical "symposium," consisting of the prologue and
the two series of speeches with the possibility that at
first there was only one series (III-XIV) results in a
sort of collective miracle that is scarcely credible.
Those, however, who have time and leisure to follow
such a process carefully will find much that is stimulating and suggestive. And at any rate we do not
find in this author any of the nonsense about fraud
and falsehood that is [2] written by those who have not
considered sufficiently the difference between ancient
and modern methods of literary composition. He says:

We must, therefore, feel grateful to those who thus
labored to change the original trend of the book, even
though they also hoped that the apparent unity given to the
elaborate compilation might remain unquestioned for all
times. Nor should we, after completing our task of undoing
the work of zealots, exchange our gratitude for condemnation of the uncritical spirit betrayed by those who thus tried
to cover the naked scepticism of the original book with an
orthodox garb. An age that has not developed the full sense
of individual authorship necessarily lacks the critical attitude towards literary production. *We* can see the intent in
the manipulations to which the text was subjected, but those
who were engaged in the endeavour saw only a perfectly
obvious measure of furnishing their superimposed interpretation of a problem that was left in an unsatisfactory state
by predecessors who had tried their hand at solving it; and
they no doubt sincerely believed that they were improving
the original production. What we would differentiate as
text and commentary, as argument and answer, as original
draft and later amplification are, in an ancient composition,
produced at a time when a literary product was regarded
as common property, to be modified and enlarged at will,
thrown together.

[2] Jastrow, p. 145.

This has been recognised in the literary criticism which has done so much to renew and enlarge the life of the Old Testament, but each case must be considered on its own merits.

2. *Peculiarities of the Book*

(*a*) *A Literary Production.* In our view this is the greatest poetic contribution by a single writer in the Old Testament, even if a quarter of it comes from later hands. As the sustained effort of a man of genius spent upon one problem it is unique. The splendid poems of the great prophets were separate pieces on a variety of topics, and were probably dependent at first on oral transmission. It is evident that we have now reached a literary age. Whatever its length the original book was a written production of considerable extent; and additions made to it were the work of students and scribes.

(*b*) *Use of Dialogue.* The sustained use of dialogue for purposes of discussion is a special feature, and this also points to a time of intellectual movement when religious problems were made the subject of elaborate debate. Conversations are reported elsewhere in histories and stories and wherever there was real life men were interested in each other's views of God and the world. But here there is a concentration and energy that speak of real study, though it is not a dry, formal argument but has the freedom and fervour of real poetry.

(*c*) *Dramatic Unity.* The way in which story and discussion is combined is found only here; when examined closely there may be only a loose connection, but it creates an interesting situation and suggests at the start an impression of dramatic unity. By the exercise

of great ingenuity expositors have managed to extract
from, or rather to read into the Song of Songs a story
as the basis of a drama of life and love, but there we
have a collection of lyrics with, at times, suggestions of
responsive songs and chorus. Here the discussion is
based upon the story, though not woven into it in any
real, organic sense.

3. The Place of the Book in Hebrew Literature

A glance at the history of interpretation shows that,
while there is no definite tradition such as that which
for centuries linked the Pentateuch with the name of
Moses, and while in ancient times there was no unanimity as to whether the man, Job, was a real or ficti-
tious character, yet there were features about the book
that suggested a very early date for its origin—as far
back as Moses or Solomon. During the last century,
however, a view of the history of the language, literature, and theology has been slowly worked out that
sets the book in the post-exilic period about 450 B.C.
or a little earlier. Like most of the Hebrew books it
comes to us without the name of its author. The
names of certain prophets we know and we have specimens of their poems but little else of that kind, most
of the Old Testament literature being nameless. But
there are certain lines of thought that help us to place
a large book in its own position, and when these con-
verge towards one period we reach a high degree of
probability.

(a) The Place in the Canon. The book is found in
the third division of the Hebrew list of sacred books
and it is likely that none of the books in the miscel-
laneous collection called "The Writings" belong, as
books, to the pre-exilic period. Parts of the Psalter

and of Proverbs may have existed earlier, but Chronicles, Ezra, Nehemiah, can be fixed in the Persian period. Daniel and Ecclesiastes are later; the beautiful story of Ruth is doubtful but cannot be very early. The position of Job in the English Bible may have been influenced by the tradition that connected "the Wisdom Literature" with the name of Solomon. The place that it holds in the Hebrew Bible harmonises with indications from other directions that it was one of the latest books to reach its present form.

(*b*) *An Intellectual Book*. Its position in this so-called "literature of wisdom" points in the same direction, as it, besides being a poem, is in a real sense an intellectual book. The intellect is involved in all thinking and acting, but there are times when it is predominant. In the historical period all types exist: the intellectual, the practical, the poetical. In early days there were "wise" men and women in Israel, but the different types were not so clearly defined as in later days. The simpler forms of story and poetry held the larger place in those days, showing the vigour and enthusiasm of youth. That this book belongs to the mature period of Judaism is quite clear; it is not lacking in evidence of strong feeling, outbursts of fierce passion, but whether we agree as to its precise nature or not we all recognise that it deals with a "problem." The wisdom of the Hebrews was a practical affair, different from the curiosity and subtlety of the Greeks. It had the defects of its qualities, and while in the light of world-history, as we see it now, we can rejoice that their supreme contribution was religious, we must admit that the pious sentiment "The fear of Yahweh, that is wisdom" might tend to check a healthy freedom of mind when interpreted in a narrow sense. The

point now is simply that our book must be placed in
a period when the small Jewish nation, cut off from
world politics, was concentrating its energies on religious subjects, and the priests and scribes were settling
into rigid rules the traditions and teachings of the past.
It is refreshing to find, at such time, the protest against
dogmatism and the claim for larger freedom. This
implies a growth of what we call "individualism," the
assertion of the rights of personal thought and conscience as against social customs and conventional
beliefs. This type of thought also has its history and
its vacillations in Israel as elsewhere. Whenever men
have reached even a primitive stage of what we call
civilization there has been a measure of individuality;
but among a simple tribal people a man is looked upon
as a part of the tribe or society in such an absolute
sense that his separateness as a "person" is almost lost
or, rather, not yet realised. "The heart knoweth its
own bitterness, and the stranger does not share in its
joy" is scarcely a primitive proverb, when the joys of
life were those shared in common and that people
should suffer together was regarded as natural.
The message of the early prophets is addressed to the
nation, though, of course, it can only become effective
through the faithfulness and honesty of the individual
citizens. Jeremiah is the first to give us a detailed
picture of the soul, oppressed by doubts and fears,
wrestling with his God. With him it is a living experience, a man struggling with fate, striving to accept
the Divine call but weighed down with a burden too
heavy for a lonely man. He too has his question, why
should a man toil all his life at a task that seems
hopeless? With Ezekiel, a man of a harder type, this
view of the separateness of the individual soul becomes

a dogma. He ignores the fact that "we are members one of another" and declares that each man receives the punishment for his own sin or the reward of his own righteousness.

(c) *The Problem of Suffering.* This has been a pressing question to many generations of men and has been met in various ways. In this regard the Hebrews were a plain, practical people and were not driven to subtle speculations of dreamy philosophy. To till the soil, live a healthy life, and then, at a good old age, to be buried in the family grave; this seemed to be man's destiny and was accepted, if not with fatalism, with patient submission. When accidents or sudden affliction caused distress, they were startled and puzzled. In a world where there were good and evil demons anything might happen, and it did not seem possible to reduce the variety of experiences to regular rules. This great question on the largest scale came into play with regard to the life of the nation. Ancient customs might linger round the life of the family, but Yahweh was clearly the God of the nation. The prophets preached the righteousness of God and the doctrine that fell with some strangeness on the ears of the common people: "You only have I known of all the families of the earth, therefore I will visit upon you all your iniquities" (Amos III. 2). This was clearly set forth by all the great prophets of the eighth century. Its terrible fulfilment, for so it was interpreted, in the downfall of Israel and the captivity of Judah, made a lasting impression. "Thus saith Yahweh of Hosts, return ye now from your evil ways, and from your evil doings; but they did not hear nor hearken unto me saith Yahweh. Your fathers, where are they? And the prophets, do they live forever?

But my words and my statutes, which I commanded
my servants the prophets, did they not overtake your
fathers?" (Zech. i. 4-6). The people were compelled
to give a sorrowful answer to this question and to
confess that in their history the words of the prophets
had been abundantly fulfilled. Thus it became a law
of life that suffering is the punishment for sin. A
great law which needed to be stated boldly whatever
qualifications it might need. It yielded the consola-
tory thought that God would eventually destroy
the heathen nations whose cruelty had filled the
world with misery. That faith has been abundantly
justified, if not in the precise form that they
expected.

When it is not a question of the nation but of the
personal experiences of pious men, seeking to maintain
their faith and integrity in spite of adverse circumstances, it comes nearer to us. One great thought
that has played an important part, viz., that of vica-
rious suffering, does not appear in our book. And when
it is most nobly expressed there is difference of opinion
as to whether its original application was national or
individual.

> He was despised, and rejected of men;
> A man of sorrows, and acquainted with grief:
> And as one from whom men hide their face
> He was despised, and we esteemed him not.
> Surely he hath borne our griefs,
> And carried our sorrows;
> Yet we did esteem him stricken,
> Smitten of God and afflicted.
> But he was wounded for our transgression,
> He was bruised for our iniquities:
> The chastisement of our peace was upon him;
> And with his stripes we are healed.

Here we have set side by side the popular idea that extreme suffering is a curse of God and the higher spiritual interpretation that it is not necessarily penal but may have a sacrificial power. The thought that men suffered with and for each other was old enough on the natural plane when the members of the clan were regarded as one flesh and blood. But here it reaches a higher level, having a deeper ethical content and a richer spiritual power.

(d) *The Problem in the Seventy-third Psalm.* This Psalm has been called "a miniature book of Job"; it deals with the same subject and is certainly a remarkable short poem. It is not a lyric or hymn in the strict sense, though it can be chanted or sung. It is not liturgical, that is, it is not directly an expression for prayer or praise, but the story of a man's experience, of his struggle with doubts concerning the righteousness of the world's government. The addition at the end in the versions makes him declare his verdict "In the gates of the daughter of Zion," but it is a personal meditation, and the change of "Israel" into "the righteous" in verse 1 is an easy one and is justified by the general tenor of the poem. But there is a calmness, a patient reasoning here which is absent from the speeches of Job. Yet, though it has a logical arrangement, it is not cold; it is suffused with deep feeling.

The poet states at the beginning the faith which with deep conviction he re-affirms at the close, so that we can say of him, as it is a case of mental conflict, a battle fought within the soul, which stops short of public expression:

> Perplext in faith, but pure in deeds,
> At last he beat his music out.
> There lives more faith in honest doubt,

Believe me, than in half the creeds.
He fought his doubts and gather'd strength;
He would not make his judgment blind,
He faced the spectres of the mind
And laid them; thus he came at length
To find a stronger faith his own;
And Power was with him in the night,
Which makes the darkness and the light,
And dwells not in the light alone.[3]

The poet traces the steps by which he was led into doubt; he marks clearly the turning point and relates each stage of the return journey until he finds himself again at home with God. In observing the course of events around him he was drifting to the conclusion that those who are unscrupulous and arrogant have the best of it. They increase in riches; they have the pleasures of life to the full. They move about with a self-satisfied air and their apparent success causes them to have many admirers and followers. Their action and demeanour suggested that honesty and righteousness were a hindrance rather than a help towards worldly prosperity. If this is true, why not proclaim it openly as a truth based on careful observation and real experience? Then comes the pause! "If I said, I will speak thus: Behold, I had dealt treacherously with the generation of thy children." We must admire the man's sense of responsibility, a doctrine that he cannot preach at least needs careful re-examination. He lifts it into the light of the sanctuary and finds that the view that he has formed though plausible is superficial. If the wicked are not always punished as swiftly as he would wish, he now remembers that they are set "in slippery places." He has a feeling that even

[3] *In Memoriam*, XCVI.

in the dark hour his God was holding him back from hasty conclusions and foolish action. He confesses that he had been stupid to think that the rewards of goodness were to be paid in the current coin of this realm and he reaches the highest of all beliefs that God Himself is the real reward of the faithful man. "Whom have I in heaven but thee? And there is none upon earth that I desire beside thee." It may be as many scholars think that he goes even further and hopes that even death cannot break this spiritual bond, this communion of the soul with God.

IV

THE BOOK AS A WORK OF ART

ART refers to form, but mere form cannot make a work of art; there must be a living soul as well as a beautiful body. So far as we can see there was, in those ancient days, no discussion, as among the Greeks, concerning art and its various forms. No rewards were to be gained, no prizes offered for excellence in literature, painting, or sculpture; their interests were in other directions. But real spiritual life, wherever it is, craves noble expression. The speeches of the great prophets cannot be classed among the utterances of rude, uncultured peoples. The power and beauty of the stories and songs is a high artistic achievement as well as a triumph of religious faith and patriotic passion. The meeting of Jacob with Esau, the reconciliation of Joseph with his brethren, David's reception of the news of Absalom's death may well be called "dramatic moments" even if we believe that the Hebrews of the canonical period did not produce a fully developed drama.

(a) *The Question of the Drama.* This question may easily become a matter merely of words unless it is set in the light of Israel's history. The names that have been used for the fragments of the story at the beginning and the conclusion—prologue and epilogue—suggest a dramatic character. The title "interlude" given to Elihu's speech seems to be a survival from the time when the book was regarded as a drama. If anything that can be set upon the stage is a drama, that condition can easily be fulfilled in the case of this book, and an impressive performance be produced. But in the life of the Hebrews the theatre played no part and this book was never meant to be acted. Some modern dramatists hold the view that "discussion" makes a real drama and "plot," or "movement" in the old sense, are not necessary; but Job is a Hebrew book and as such it has to be considered.

Nor is it unique merely as an exotic that has its own well-defined class elsewhere. It is, for example, no more similar to Greek or any other epic or drama than to other works of Hebrew literature. A drama in any strict sense it certainly is not; in the Prologue there is movement indeed, but the Prologue is narrative,—an anticipation of the novel rather than the drama—and in the dialogue there is no dramatic movement. There are in the book it is true all the elements that might have been combined by a Greek into a great drama; the Hebrew writer has used them differently, and his work was certainly never acted in ancient Judah.[1]

The following words, from a recent book, give the view of a distinguished Old Testament scholar.

The Book has been called a Drama and offered as proof that the Hebrews at last achieved one of the great dramas of literature, if not the greatest of all. And indeed, its use, like Shakespeare's of the frame of an old story, its delivery of dialogues between contrasted characters and the vividness in which these characters gradually but passionately reveal themselves, might justify the designation. Yet the speeches are rather separate poems than parts of dialogues, though woven into a dramatic whole round the conduct and fate of a single personality and the confronting of his soul with the power of Deity. But it is really indifferent how we define the form of the Book of Job. There Hebrew poetry,

[1] *Int. C. C.*, Vol. I, p. xxII.

scattering on its flight its richest treasures of reflection and music, soars to its highest glory.[2]

In the small land situated between the two great civilizations of Egypt and Babylonia the Hebrew contribution to the religious life of the world was formed, and though influenced by both it was not dominated by either. In the region of art its independence was clearly seen; when once the monotheistic tendency got into full swing its effect was to make plastic art impossible, and, so far as it was intelligently accepted, to clear out the element of magic from religious worship. Because of the original simplicity and severity of their life, and the fact that it was their destiny to fight against a sensuous worship and an attractive idolatry, the Hebrews were limited in what we call the artistic and aesthetic side of life. Statuary, painting and the drama were not to be in the line of their development, as they must pay the price of being specialists in a different sphere.

A more serious gap is left by the absence of drama, perhaps the greatest of all literary forms, at any rate the form in which some of the world's greatest work has been done in ancient and modern times. The genius of the Hebrew was essentially subjective, not creative. Hence there is nothing in Old Testament Literature to compare with Sophocles or Shakespeare. Such dramatic power as the Hebrews possessed is shown in narrative, in passages in the prophets and specially in Job. The last named is indeed often regarded as fundamentally a drama. But here religious speculation takes the place of plot interest, while the characterization is slight, the friends of Job not being sharply individualised, and there is a marked lack of consistency between the Job of the Prologue and the Colloquies.[3]

[2] Sir George Adam Smith, *The Legacy of Israel*, p. 26.
[3] Professor Hudson in Peake's *Commentary*.

When we go far enough back we find similarities between the religious customs and festivals of different nations, but the character of what grew out of these depended on the individual culture and special religious genius of the particular nation. It is important to remember that the Book of Job was written at a time when the Jews had reached strict monotheism that was losing some of its national features and the conflicts through which this monotheism was reached were a hindrance to the growth of a drama of the Greek type even if their genius had been in that direction.

A dramatic character belongs even to the cultus, the festive processions and dances, certainly also to many rites which the pilgrim-shrines had to take part in,—a liturgy making use of questions and answers (Ps. xxiv) and those songs, mostly improvised, in which leader and choir performed alternately. If here those taking part do so in their own proper persons, the women who yearly bewailed the daughter of Jephthah (Judg. xi. 39) played the part of another, and the same is true of the mourning women when they raised the common cry, "Ah, my brother!" "Ah, my Lord" (Jer. xxii. 18), and every wedding was a small drama.[4]

There is more than one reason why these "germs" did not grow into the direction of the drama; an important one, if not the chief, being the monotheistic movement which ruled out heroes and demi-gods from the higher literature.

Among the Greeks the drama sprang from two sources, the religious festivals, specially those of Dionysius, the god of wine and love, and the ancient mythology found in its noblest form in the Homeric stories. The dithyramb or dance chorus is the ances-

[4] B. Duhm.

tor of the tragic drama; but it is a long story which
tells us how a celebration in which all took part was
gradually turned into performance at which the actors
were few and the spectators many; it belongs to the
story of Greece and scholars have delighted in tracing
the process step by step and seeking to discover and
estimate the separate contributions of the great poets.

In tracing the origin and growth of the primitive drama,
the point which impresses itself most forcibly upon the
attention is the gradual and tentative character of its early
progress.   The invention of the drama like many other
human discoveries so far from being achieved by sudden
inspiration was the result of a protracted series of innova-
tions and experiments, of which the eventual tendency was
for a long time far from manifest.   The hesitating manner
in which the ancient poets proceeded with the work of development, and the slowness with which they gradually came
to realise the varied capacities of the new form, may at first
sight cause surprise.   Theatrical performances have now
become so familiar to the mind that we are apt to regard
them as an obvious and natural contrivance, and to under-
rate the merit of those by whom they were originally discovered.[5]

(b) *Mythology in the Book of Job.*   When we
remember that reminiscences of mythology linger long
in poetry, it is remarkable how little of it there is in
this book.

Lo! let that night be barren evermore,
And let no sound of joy be heard therein;
Who curse the day, let them forever curse it,
They who are ready to rouse Leviathan.   (III. 7, 8.)

Here there is reference to ancient and wide-spread
belief still to be found in many lands that in an eclipse
a great dragon was seeking to swallow the sun or moon.

[5] A. S. Haigh, *The Tragic Drama of the Greeks,* p. 10.

Whether there is an allusion to the great "chaos-dragon" of Babylonian mythology is doubtful. Whether Leviathan in XLI. 1 has any mythological significance is also uncertain.

Am I a sea, a monster of the deep?
That thou should'st o'er me watch. (VII. 12.)

To us the words suggest merely that the God of Israel created the world and rules the restless sea. So far shall the mighty ocean come, but at the limit set by the divine decree its "proud waves" shall be stayed (XXXVIII. 11). But the reference to the sea monster is a reminiscence of the old Babylonian myth.

Through His power the sea was stilled;
And by His understanding He smote through Rahab;
By His wind the heavens are brightened;
His hand pierceth the fleeing serpent. (XXVI. 12, 13.)

Here the text is more difficult (cf. Isaiah XXVII. 1, a passage which in the manner of Apocalypse, speaks of the future in this imagery drawn from the past; and Isaiah LI. 9, where the mighty acts of the past are called for in the present). Many scholars find here as in IX. 13, "allusions to the Hebrew form (in which all creative activity was attributed to Yahweh) of the old Babylonian mythological account of the creation." When our book was written the stars had, for the Hebrews, ceased to be regarded as gods. In Genesis I they are creatures of Israel's God, "he made the stars also"; the poet of the exile says: "Lift up your eyes on high, and behold who hath created these?" Yet in this splendid couplet there is a reminiscence of the old view:

When the morning stars sang together,
And all the sons of God shouted for joy. (XXXVIII. 7.)

If all such allusions were carefully examined we would still be impressed with the soberness as well as the freedom of the poet.

(c) *The Story*. The first two chapters are a fine specimen of simple Hebrew prose, rising at the crucial points into poetic form.

> Naked from my mother's womb I came,
> And naked there shall I again return;
> Yahweh gave, and Yahweh hath taken away,
> Yahweh's name be blessed.   (I. 21.)

It is probable, though not certain, that the story was in existence before the poems were written; the fact that its connection with the other parts of the book is so slight points in this direction. It may have contained some discussion of the problems but that is uncertain. As it stands it makes a good introduction to the dialogues. We do not know the origin or the meaning of the name Job. Long ago Jewish scholars debated as to whether he "existed" or not, and were not unanimous in their views. It is a *true* story, whoever wrote it, if we mean by that a picture of real life. Sudden changes come to men in ways that they cannot explain. And there is no greater test of character than a quick change of circumstances in the direction of poverty and pain, or of unexpected increase of riches and popularity. This is not dependent on the photographic accuracy of the picture—the great thing in Scripture interpretation is to grasp the principles involved. Truths that the Jews learned through symbols and presented as the arbitrary action of God, regarded as absolute monarch, we set forth as revelations gained through human experience. The ancients said, "Whom the gods wish to destroy they first make mad." We see things that call the proverb to mind, but we dwell more on the human side and regard the sudden catastrophes as the result of that jealousy, pride, and arrogance which sometimes blind men of great ability in their hour of success.

People forget this who talk about Job being "arbitrarily handed over to the tender mercies of Satan." *The* Satan is not the Devil of later theology. There is a tremendous difference between Satan in Paradise Lost and the Satan in the book of Job. The former is a prince, leader of the false gods and devils who are united in defying the Lord of heaven and earth, seeking to scatter sin and shame over the peaceful earth. Milton's Satan is heroic, defiant, more like Prometheus of the Greek play than the critic or opponent that we meet in this simple story. Here again we must pay attention to the history of the name and the idea. *Satan* in its verbal form means "to hinder, to oppose"; Numbers XXII. 22, "The angel of Yahweh set himself in the way to resist him"; verse 32, "and the angel said . . . I went out to withstand thee." The noun means an enemy in war, I Sam. XXIX. 4, "lest in the battle he be an adversary (*satan*) to us." In a court of law, Psalm CIX. 6, 7, here instead of Satan we should have adversary:

> Set a wicked man over him;
> And let an adversary stand at his right hand.
> When he shall be judged let him be condemned;
> And let his prayer become sin.

In Zechariah III. 1, we have both noun and verb in the same sentence, "the opponent stood up to oppose him." It leads to confusion to give in English "the Satan," neither is it correct to leave out the article. In I Chronicles XXI. 1, there is no article and the word is clearly used as a proper name, "Satan," who appears

in the rôle of tempter or seducer. In II Samuel xxiv.
1, it is said that Yahweh did tempt David, but here
four or five centuries later that expression is objectionable and Satan plays this devilish part. In this
story the *satan* or adversary is not a tempter but a
cynical critic. In certain ecclesiastical courts if a person is brought up for the formal conferring of the
title "saint" there is an *advocatus diaboli*, a critic or
opponent who brings up all that can be said on the
opposite side. This, if carefully done, is a wise pre-
caution for those who bestow canonical honours. In
our story one of the sons of God or angels assumes this
office and seems to have a malicious pleasure in it, as
he demands that the test shall be pushed to the limit
of human endurance; everything must go except life
itself to prove that Job's religion is not a matter of
self-interest. Job stands the test and has lived in
history as "the patient Job." This critic and censor
then disappears from the scene having played his part.

(*d*) *The Discussion.* At this stage the poet introduces the great controversy which opens with Job's
wild complaints standing in such strong contrast to
what has gone before. If we cannot accept the view
that a popular pre-existing book has been used, we
must explain the situation from the fact that when
speech comes after long and severe repression it is
likely to be passionate and violent. Job curses the
day in which he was born, complains that he was
allowed to live, and wishes that death would now come
to one who would hail it as a welcome visitor. This
gives the impulse to the discussion that is carried on
through several chapters; each of the friends in turn
replies to Job's complaints. There is no impersona-
tion; each man represents himself, and all "the friends"

represent the orthodox doctrines that the wicked are punished and the righteous rewarded, and that with regard to the moral government of the world no just complaint can be made against God. Such problems had engaged the thoughts of men in earlier ages and in other lands, but there is no need to think of direct influence or "borrowing" in the crude sense. We are told that Aeschylus the great Greek dramatist was at the same period handling similar problems, but the material, style and atmosphere were very different. The punishment of sin, the power of fate, the innocent sufferers involved with the guilty, the curse on the father passing down to the children, all these thoughts are presented in the ancient tragedies in sublime poetry and with gloom and horror that gave real meaning to the word "tragic." The following quotations from this great artist may remind us of sentences in the Book of Job, but the world in which the Greek poet lives, with its luxuriant and complicated mythologies, is different from that of the simple community that was growing up in and around Jerusalem.

Zeus inclines the scales on either side, sending evil to the wicked, good to the just. "It is an old saying that much prosperity begets misfortune." I hold a creed far apart from this. It is the impious deed that brings forth an offspring of woe, like its parent stock. But the house that loves justice shall flourish from generation to generation. For Zeus has appointed that "suffering should bring instruction" and "it is a good thing to be taught wisdom by misfortune." [6]

But it is pointed out that in the Promethus Bound, a drama which some have tried to connect with Job, a lower idea of Zeus is given; he is there the representa-

[6] Haigh, p. 94.

tive of brute force and selfish despotism; sympathy and humanity are the qualities of Prometheus.[7] Nowhere else in the Old Testament do we find the spirit of revolt to the same extent as in the speeches of Job. The Hebrew mind tended to submissiveness and fatalism in the presence of God (cf. Ps. xxxix). We can imagine Job startling and shocking "the friends" with the bold words, "My head is bloody but unbowed."

We may then call the dialogue dramatic, though the book is not in the fullest sense a drama. The men, Eliphaz, Bildad and Zophar, are not very clearly differentiated, though they are roughly individualized. The first is the eldest, "older than Job's father," and can speak of revelations that have come to him; the second makes his appeal to tradition and the proverbial wisdom of his people; Zophar, the youngest, shows more rudeness and impetuosity of speech. As they are meant to support one another and to preach similar views, we cannot expect any very striking differences in their style.

There is one thing that might be expected and that can be clearly traced, that is, that as the controversy is continued the contestants drift, or are driven, farther apart. The gentle tone of the beginning is lost; impatience and bitterness increase. This is one of the dangers of "controversy." Reasonable discussion may be stimulating and helpful; men may lead each other to clearer views when there is some measure of sympathy, but when the clash of opinions comes from positions too far apart heat rather than light is produced. At first Job appears to the friends to be simply unfortunate, but when he utters his despairing cries his wickedness is proved by his lack of faith and patience.

[7] P. 112.

The range of this subject also grows; it begins with Job's personal suffering and passes out into the larger region of world-government. Though it is so much a personal question it is possible that the background of the nation's life, with its sorrows and failures, makes itself felt. That Judah with the supreme God and the true religion should suffer and be enslaved by foreigners was a problem for the faithful worshippers; but in this period the question of the apparent prosperity of the wicked within their own community caused concern to the strict observers of the Law, and it was not always easy to maintain the simple faith of the first Psalm that the good prosper and the wicked waste away.

It was not simply the problem of pain, though that in its extreme form is hard to bear, but of the meaning of life as a whole. We know that pain has its uses and that in this world we cannot expect a life of unbroken ease and a pathway that is always smooth. In the light of Christian hope we may sing these brave, beautiful words; it is easier, however, to sing them when we are free from pain:

> I thank Thee more that all our joy
> Is touched with pain,
> That shadows fall on brightest hours,
> That thorns remain;
> So that earth's bliss may be our guide,
> And not our chain,
> For Thou, Who knowest, Lord, how soon
> Our weak heart clings,
> Hast given us joys, tender and true
> Yet all with wings,
> So that we see, gleaming on high
> Diviner things.[8]

[8] A. A. Proctor.

It is certain that in Job's case the pain is represented as severe, almost intolerable, and this is the
cause of his rash or incoherent speech. To this is
added the mental torture of being misunderstood and
having to listen to irritating platitudes that have no
power to console. He rejects with scorn their claim to
speak for God:

> But ye, indeed! forgers of lies are ye;
> Physicians of no value are ye all.
> O that you would be altogether still.
> For that would surely be your wisest way.
>
> (XIII. 4, 5.)

Along this line no solution can be reached. The argument sways backward and forward but with no real
movement towards a satisfactory close. It is a brilliant debate in which many striking things, truths and
half-truths, are said on both sides, but if we were left
with nothing more than these speeches there would
be not only no solution but nothing to relieve the bitterness of strife or to ease in any way the sufferer's
burden. Pictures of life are here from many points of
view; many moods find vivid expression. A rigid dogmatism and a despairing scepticism meet in fierce strife
but fail to reach a common faith.

V

JOB'S POSITION

Though, as we have said, the discussion ranges over a large field, in examining the significance of misfortune the personality of this one man stands out distinctly and in defending his integrity and freedom from serious offences that would justify the treatment he has received he draws on his own experience and presents clearly his ideal of "the just man" (XXXI). He is a man who, in the meantime, has lost his God. The situation is expressed in the cry:

> Oh, that I knew where I might find Him,
> That I might come even to His seat!
> I would order my cause before Him,
> And fill my mouth with arguments.   (XXIII. 3.)

What could he think or do when there seemed to be no answer to his persistent cry and he was constantly reminded that the reason was not in God but in himself.

(a) He could not deny God's existence; that would have been to reject the sober faith that Judaism had achieved after long conflicts with idolatry. "For every house is builded by someone; but He that built all things is God" (Heb. III. 4): that had become for men of intelligence a solid conviction. A man might say in his heart, "There is no God"; that is, act as if God took no interest in men's conduct, but "atheism" whatever that may mean, is a later growth, the product of an artificial intellectualism. The painful thing was that Job believed that God was there, but that he could not see or hear Him as he had once done.

> O that it were with me as in the moons of old;
> As in the days when o'er me still Eloah watched,
> When shone His lamp above my head,
> And when through darkness by His light I walked.
>
> (XXIX. 2, 3.[1])

His darkest hour was when he was driven to think of God as an arbitrary lord who by brute force scattered confusion among the creatures whom he had created. But he still believed that God was in the centre of things and, as a reaction after his bitterest speeches a faint streak of light would struggle through the dark clouds and he would hope that there was some explanation.

> I falter where I firmly trod,
> And falling with my weight of cares
> Upon the great world's altar stairs
> That slope thro' darkness up to God
> I stretch lame hands of faith, and grope,
> And gather dust and chaff, and call
> To what I feel is Lord of all,
> And faintly trust the larger hope.[2]

(b) It is true that Job longed for death, that he prayed for release from his suffering:

[1] Dean Inge (Outspoken Essays, p. 177) speaking of Cardinal Newman's depression, at a certain period of his career, quotes from one of his letters this passage—of course in the Latin, "Quis mihi tribuat, ut sim juxta menses pristinos, secundum dies, quibus Deus custodiebat me? Quando splendebat lucerna ejus super caput meum, et ad lumen ejus ambulabam in tenebris?"

[2] In Memoriam, LV.

> O that my prayer were heard;
> That God would grant the thing for which I long.
> Let him consent and crush me down;
> Let loose his hand and cut my thread of life.
>
> (v. 19.)

But it is not likely that he meditated cutting the thread of life with his own hand. The ancient stoics and others have regarded that course as an honourable retiral from defeat and shame. Dr. Dillon, reviving the view held by earlier scholars, thinks that he faced this alternative: "This request having been refused, suicide, the ever 'open door' of the Stoics, invited him temptingly in, but he withstood the temptation and comforted himself with the knowledge that all things in time have an end:

> " 'My soul would have chosen strangling
> And death by my own resolve.
> But I spurned it; for I shall not live forever.' "

But unfortunately there is difficulty in the translation of these lines. There is pretty general agreement as to the first two lines:

> So that my soul chooseth strangling,
> And death rather than these pains. (VII. 15.)

and several variations as to the third line: "I refuse it (i.e. my life) not forever would I live"; "I refuse to live any longer"; "I have lost all hope of being able to live longer"; or, changing the order slightly, "I despise death in the presence of my pains."

In any case it was not "a way out" for Job, whether or not he had learned that the Almighty had "fixed a canon against self-slaughter." At this stage one could not expect such subtle and elaborate treatment as Shakespeare gives it when he represents Hamlet as balancing the ills of the present against those that we know not of, concluding that conscience doth make cowards of us all, so that "the native hue of resolution is sicklied o'er with the pale cast of thought and enterprises of great pith and moment turn awry and lose the name of action." Job is no coward; he does not shrink from contemplating death and while there is no attraction in the regions beyond, he thinks that it cannot be worse than the torment of the present. The thoughts of a young man full of life and bent on sensual pleasure facing the certain destiny of the body and the uncertain future of the spirit are forcefully expressed in the words of Claudio:

> 'tis too horrible!
> The weariest and most loathed earthly life
> That age, ache, penury and imprisonment
> Can lay on nature, is a paradise
> To what we fear of death.[3]

The Hebrew as he approached the natural end of life regarded death with serenity and to a man in Job's position with all its mystery it had a certain attraction.

(c) In the literature of post-exilic Judaism there are two books that are not touched by the national hopes of an early deliverance which would usher in "the reign of the saints," Job and Ecclesiastes. In the latter book the scepticism is calm with a touch of that cynical spirit that fears fanaticism and enthusiasm most of all. In Job there is passion and energy; he has in his own way the prophetic spirit, but there is an element of what for want of a better name we may call "rationalism." Job seeks to stand face to face with God. He does not show the characteristics of a later

[3] *Measure for Measure.*

and lower Judaism which Dean Inge describes in such definite terms:

As God was raised above direct contact with men, the old animistic belief in angels and demons, which had lasted on in the popular mind by the side of the worship of Yahweh was extended in a new way. A celestial hierarchy was invented, with names, and an infernal hierarchy too; the malevolent ghosts of animism became fallen angels. Satan, who in Job is the crown prosecutor, one of God's retinue, becomes God's adversary; and the angels, formerly manifestations of God himself, are now quite separated from Him.[4]

This side of Jewish theology does not concern us here directly, as Job ignores it, but as the writer just quoted points out it had in it a real element of religious faith:

The apocalyptic prophecies of post-Exilic Judaism, which were not based, like some political predictions of the earlier prophets on a statesmanlike view of the international situation, but on hopes of supernatural intervention, had their roots in visions of a new and better world-order. This aspiration, which had to disentangle itself by degrees from the patriotic dreams of a stubborn and unfortunate race, was projected into the near future, and was mixed with less worthy political ambitions which had a different origin. The prophet always foreshortens his revelation, and generally blends the City of God with a vision of his own country transfigured.

(d) The most powerful consolation against the thought that life is short and often painful is the confident belief or strong hope that there is a brighter prospect beyond the grave. Such a belief was held by many Jews at a later time but Job, though he faces the question, could not attain a steady, unwavering hope. He has the view common in his day, but one difficult for us to define and understand, of the under-

[4] *Outspoken Essays*, pp. 215, 247.

world of the dead, peopled with shadowy figures who live but do not possess any of the joys or pains of the earthly life. Death is the great leveller but it is a dead level of negation and monotony.

> For there the wicked cease their raging;
> There the weary are at rest;
> There lie the captives all at ease;
> The driver's voice they hear no more.
> The small and great alike are there,
> The servant from his master free. (III. 17-19.)

But Job does try to pierce through this gloom to something brighter beyond, not by any dark superstitious methods, but rather by a living faith that clings to the conviction that there is a real spiritual relation between God and the man whom he has created. Unfortunately just at the most important places there are difficulties in the text especially in the great passage beginning, "I know that my Vindicator liveth," etc. We have to remember that we are dealing not with a dogmatic treatise but with poetry that represents varying moods and delicate shades of feeling. When he has dwelt upon the figure of a sprouting tree, which, after it has been cut down has a kind of resurrection, and declared, "But man dies and passes away," he cannot get rid of the question, "If a man dies will he live again" (XIV. 14.).

> So man lies down to rise no more,
> Until the Heavens be gone they ne'er awake,
> Nor start them from their sleep.
> Oh that in Sheol thou wouldest lay me up,
> That thou would'st hide me till thy wrath shall turn,
> Set me a time and then remember me.

If Job denies so strongly that man can have hope of survival after death, yet the example of the tree has

cast a thought into his soul which is too attractive for him
not to linger upon it for a moment. He cannot yet hold
it fast, but the suggestion which lies in the contrast between
the tree and man, and which increases still further by his
hyperbole, leads us to conjecture that behind the strong
rejection of survival there is hidden the inclination to
believe in it.[5]

The difficulties of translating and explaining each sentence in the great passage xix. 25-27, are so great that
there is never likely to be unanimity with regard to it.
But there is glimmering through the darkness the hope
that after death his integrity will be vindicated by God
and that he will have a vision of his God no longer
estranged from him; but while his hopes may have
helped men to a clearer faith in this direction they cannot be regarded as the solution of the great problem.

[5] B. Duhm

VI

THE SPIRITUAL SIGNIFICANCE
OF THE BOOK

As the Elihu speeches have no real connection with
the rest of the book we pass from the discussions to the
speech of the Almighty which shows the same ener-
getic movement and sublime style as the speeches of
Job. This used to be called a "theophany," that is an
appearance of God, and compared with the manifes-
tation of God in the thunderstorm in the ancient literature. But here the storm is a part of the literary
form. This is not so much an appearance in the world
of nature as a revelation in the mind of the poet. He
turns for a while away from the close atmosphere in
which all his thoughts were centred on himself and his
own sufferings. From the world of men with their continued and fruitless controversies he turns to the great
world, its greatness, its splendours and its mysteries.
Here he finds not a specific answer to his questionings
but a larger outlook, a suggestion that the God who
moves in a mysterious way is wiser than himself. He
has asked many questions; now the questioning spirit
turns inward as he looks out upon the wonders of the
lofty heaven and the boundless earth. In view of our
modern science, some of the questions may seem simple enough, but the sense of mystery that they pro-
voked is just as real in the dark fringe of our wider
knowledge. Our difficulties spring from the larger

view of the world that is forced upon us by the immense extent of time and space that confronts us. The principle that man is not the centre of the world begins to make itself felt; the universe is larger than our personal experiences; our sorrows and failures cannot be made a complete measure of God's wisdom and goodness. "He describes in God's speech with a certain enthusiasm, we may say, with exultation, the glorious wonder of the world, and the wonders in the world. He rejoices that his God, Whose righteousness he cannot recognize in human destiny, although he does not doubt its existence, shows and has shown in creation "counsel" and greatness; only man can go no further than that he both feels and dimly glimpses it, he cannot comprehend it. Thus this poet whose realism even here is not surrendered boldly grasps the bull by the horns; the world is wonderful and glorious, but it is a riddle—so let it be a riddle! It is the piety of the sceptic that speaks to us in these speeches. And finally there is a God, and Job may see him. The Vision of God reconciles him to his sufferings and problems; he throws them from him and will die gladly because he has seen God." [1] If we call this "scepticism" we must admit that it is better than a stagnant, conventional creed, and it certainly shows more of the religious spirit in its treatment of nature than "The Preacher," as may be seen by comparing the following passages:

One generation goeth, and another cometh;
And the earth abideth forever.
The sun arises and the sun goes down,
And hastens to the place where he arises
The wind goeth toward the south,

[1] B. Duhm.

And turneth about unto the north.
It turneth about continually in its course,
And the wind returneth again to its circuits.
All the rivers run into the sea,
And yet the sea is not full.
Unto the place whither the rivers go,
Thither they go again.
All words are wearisome
Men cannot utter it in words
The eye is not satisfied with seeing,
Nor the ear filled with hearing.
That which hath been is that which shall be,
And that which hath been done is that which shall be done,
And there is nothing new under the sun.   (Eccles. i. 4-9.)

How different this depressing view of a man weary
with the "never-ceasing whirl" compared with Job's
enthusiasm over a world that is alive with the presence
and power of the eternal God.

Say, where wast thou when earth's deep base I laid?
Declare it if thy science goes so far.
Who fixed its measurements that thou should'st know;
Or on it stretched the line?
On what were its foundations sunk?
Who laid its corner stone?
When morning stars in chorus sang;
And cried aloud for joy, the sons of God.   (xxxviii. 6.)

The speech of the Almighty of which this is the beginning shows a sympathy with nature as the manifes-
tation of God's power and wisdom; if it does not solve
our moral problems it draws us into a sphere where we
forget for a while not merely petty cares, but where
even some of the more oppressive burdens of life are
lightened.

It is appropriate that after this should come Job's
repentance and submission (xl. 4, 5; xlii. 5, 6) his
final word; as "the happy ending" with worldly com-

pensation stands outside his scheme of thought. The personal problem is solved in so far as he is prepared to trust the goodness of God, even where he cannot trace it in all the events of his own life. It is solved not by arguments but by a larger vision of God, by the conviction that all through the darkness and in spite of his wild wandering cries God was with him. It is still a personal question; theories and speculations as to whether this is the best of all possible worlds have little practical bearing. He did not claim to be competent to settle the general question of God's government of the world, but he did give expression to the doubts and perplexities that assail the soul of the man who is called to suffer greatly. If he could have found a formula that met the need of his time and justified the ways of God to man it would soon have been out of relation with actual life and thought. If we read the speech of the Almighty in its orginal form, in a spirit of simplicity and sympathy, we shall feel the fresh breezes and realise that out in the wider spaces of God's world there is something that rebukes our impatience and our pride.

It has been said, with much truth, that the book is a protest against making sin the chief or only explanation of suffering. There is no one key that unlocks all the doors. God fulfils himself in many ways lest one good custom or one rigid dogma should corrupt the world. The view that suffering is the punishment for sin was, as we have seen, an advance on the more primitive view; it did bring some semblance of order into man's moral life. But when applied in a narrow Pharisaic spirit without careful qualification it became both false and cruel. We are told that the modern man is not much concerned about "sin"; that he is tempted

to regard it as a theological term that has lost its
meaning, if it ever had any. Whether such lack of
concern is to be regarded as a sign of superiority or of
superficiality might call forth different answers. If
true, it would mean that much of the language of the
Old Testament, of Paul, Augustine, Luther, Bunyan,
and other "saints" has become foreign and so, for us,
antiquated. Penitential psalms and other literature
that pictures man face to face with God would have
lost their power of appeal to the human soul. Crime
we understand, as it means the wilful breaking of laws
made by man for the welfare of society, some of which,
if we have any faith at all, we must regard as ordinances of God. How far each element of justice (not
mere vengeance) prevention, and reformation should
play their part needs careful consideration. Even here
the innocent may suffer because our administration of
justice is imperfect. There are cases where there is
no court of appeal for the innocent except God. When
we come into the presence of God we like Job may
find it difficult to maintain our innocence. To regard
the sense of sin, remorse, repentance, and the cry for
mercy as artificial products of a conventional religion,
or as shadowy survivals from a superstitious age is
probably neither a true nor a noble view. But Job's
protest against treating suffering mainly as punishment
is amply justified.

The following striking passage has recently come to
my notice:

The stage and the personages selected are only the out-
ward signs of an inward spiritual revolution; the bold
efforts to win the way out of religious provincialism into
that world of the spirit, of which men of every tribe and
race are natives and citizens. In effecting this advance the

author develops what, as we have seen, Hebrew prophets had already maintained, the right of the individual soul to measure its experience of life against doctrines of the divine justice. He articulates more clearly the protests of Psalmists and others against the dogma that human suffering is proof of human guilt; yet discards not only rigid doctrines of retribution but *all* human attempts to define the Divine will and duty. Never has the inadequacy of these attempts been so powerfully exposed in face of the infinite power and inscrutable wisdom of God as revealed in Creation. The author's ethical insight and skill in the analysis of character is conspicuous in his conception of his hero as afflicted not only by physical distresses but by the sorer agony of having his honesty questioned and his character torn up by those who had been his friends; yet there is equal power in showing how so terrible a fate is discipline, stirring a man to deeper knowledge of himself, without further attempt to solve the problems raised—a reserve which is itself a mark of power—in describing Job's ultimate repentance and surrender to God.[2]

The glory of this book is that it has preserved for us in such a splendid form the story of one of the noblest efforts to maintain the freedom of the soul and the right of the individual to appeal directly to the throne of God. In these days the talk about "living our own life," "expressing ourselves" is in danger of becoming a fashionable cant. It is true that in every age we are saved from dead conventionality and tyrannical traditions by those who seek to see things as they are and to translate everlasting truth into the language of their own time. But doing this is one thing, and merely talking about it is another. In reading the words of Job we feel that we are face to face with reality. The Judaism that kept alive the religion, that built the new temple, that preserved the

[2] Sir G. A. Smith, *The Legacy of Israel*, p. 27.

book, and handed down the traditions, rendered a need-
ful and noble service, but it had its dangers. As in
other ages when men have been fighting for their religion and their lives, there was hardness and intoler-
ance, but a community that kept among its sacred
treasures, even by means that seem strange to us, such
books as Job, Jonah, and Ecclesiastes, that show a
spirit remarkable for its breadth and boldness, must
be admitted to have had some "catholicity." We may
think that Job's testimony, his cry for liberty, is not
needed now when we have attained so much freedom,
and that what we need is a deeper sense of responsibility to our God and to our fellow men. Yet the time
is not likely to come, at least not within any period that
we need to reckon with, when this union of the free
spirit with the religious temper will be out of date.
This wonderful combination of freedom and faith will
keep it alive when many "epoch-making" books have
passed into oblivion. It does not come within the
range of our purpose to review the problem of pain as
it has been affected by the thought of later times and
the influence of the Christian revelation, but we may
close with the words of one who as a scholar and
preacher, having pondered long on the teaching of the
book, gave his message from a central position:[3]

The light given in this book was dim and scanty. We
see in it the dawn of one of those new and healing truths
fragments of which are flashed upon the human soul in
hours of pain. But we see the dawn only. The effect of
the teaching on the Jewish Church was clearly small. Men
still needed, centuries later, to be warned against looking
for special judgment in the fall of a tower, in the merci-
lessness of a Roman governor (Luke XIII. 1-4). More, far

[3] Westminster Abbey.

more, was needed to complete the teaching which the story of Job had inaugurated. The whole revelation of the Christian life—the upward course of One who was "made perfect through suffering"—has brought a new idea into the world, one whose future fullness is only indicated and fore-shadowed in this book. But it was one which the age of Job could hardly have conceived, and which centuries later the Jewish nation steadfastly rejected. It has leavened race after race with the ennobling sense that, as this great tale, as this "flower of Old Testament poetry" has its roots in sorrow, so the highest, the divinest life may be compatible with sorrow, may rest on pain and self-sacrifice. To how many sufferers has the lesson come like spring airs to a frozen soil—taught them that the truest use of pain, yea sometimes of spiritual pain, and racking doubts and disturbing questions, is not to paralyse but to strengthen the soul, to brace us to do good work for God and man.[4]

[4] Dean Bradley, p. 332.

VII

SELECTIONS FROM THE ORIGINAL BOOK OF JOB

Two points must be made clear—first, that the passages in this section are chosen from those parts of the book generally admitted to be genuine, and second, the translation does not claim to be a new one. In the American edition of Lange's Commentary,[1] 1874, there is "A Rhythmical Version with Introduction and Annotations," into which the author, Professor Tayler Lewis, LL.D., Union College, Schenectady, New York, put a great deal of careful critical work. In many cases this scholar seems to me to have been successful in giving a rhythm which, if not exactly that of the original, suggests its poetic spirit. I have used this *freely* but, as, in the course of fifty years light has been thrown upon many points, I have consulted as well as the public versions, many commentaries and critical discussions. The student who desires minute exegesis must look elsewhere, as all that is attempted here is to catch the general line of discussion, and to make the substance of the book available for those who cannot devote much time to special studies.

1. *Chapter iii*

With this chapter we may, with advantage, compare Jeremiah's treatment of a similar subject, written probably more than a century earlier. The prophet fought

---

[1] "Job," by Otto Zöcklen, D.D.

a fierce battle in circumstances that are fairly well known to us. The political life of the nation was breaking down and its religious affairs were in confusion. In this passage we have the words wrung from the heart of a man who was fighting a noble battle against fearful odds:

Cursed be the day on which I was born;
  The day on which my mother bare me—
    Let it not be blessed!
Cursed be the man who brought glad tidings to my father,
  Saying: "A son is born to thee."
    Making him glad.

Let that man be like the cities
Which Yahweh overthrew without pity;
Let him hear a cry in the morning,
And an alarm at noon;
Because he slew me not from the womb,

That my mother might have been my grave.
And her womb always great,
Why came I out of the womb,
To see trouble and sorrow,
That my days should be spent in shame?

Job's curse is more elaborate and artistic yet it is not artificial; there is real feeling throbbing through it and in many of its lines it has a wonderful beauty and strength.

(a.) *He Wishes That He Had Not Been Born*

1. Perish the day in which I was to be born
     The night that said, Behold a man-child.
3-4. That day! O be it darkness evermore;
     Eloah never seek it from above,
     Nor ever shine the light upon its face
5. Let darkness and deep gloom reclaim it,
     Dense clouds upon it make their fixed abode,
     And dire eclipses fill it with affright.

6. That night! Thick darkness take it for its own,
   In the years' reckoning may it never joy;
   Nor come into the number of the months.

7. Lo! let that night be barren evermore,
   And let no sound of joy be heard therein

8. Who curse the day, let them forever curse it—
   They who stand ready to rouse Leviathan.

9. Be dark its twilight stars.
   For light let it look forth, and look in vain;
   Nor may it ever see the eyelids of the dawn.

10. For that it did not shut the womb when I was born,
    Nor hide the coming sorrow from mine eyes.

(b.) *He Wishes That He Had Died at Birth*

11. Why at the birth did I not die?
    When from the womb I came and breathe my last?

12. Why were the nursing knees prepared?
    And why the breast that I should suck?

13. For then in silence I had lain me down
    Yea, I had slept and been at rest.

16. Or like the hidden birth had never lived;
    Like still-born babes that never saw the light.

17. For there the wicked cease their raging
    There the weary are at rest.

18. There lie the captives all at ease;
    The driver's voice they hear no more.

19. The small and great alike are there.
    The servant from his master free.

(c.) *Asks Why Life Should Be Continued to Men Whose Suffering Leads Them to Desire Death*

20. O why does He give light to one in pain?
    Or life to the embittered soul?

21. To those who long for death that never comes,
    Who seek for it beyond the search for treasure;

22. Who joy to exultation,—yea
    Are very glad when they can find the grave.

23. (The grave) 'tis for the man whose way is hid,
    Whom God hath hedged around.

25. For I did greatly fear and it hath come;
    Yea it hath come to me, the thing that was my dread;
26. For I was not at ease, nor felt secure,
    Nor rested thoughtlessly, yet trouble came.

2. *Chapters iv-v*

The first speech of Eliphaz, the Temanite, begins
with gentle remonstrance reminding Job that one who
has seen sorrow come to others and shown sympathy
with the sufferers should not be surprised if he is called
to bear his share. Surely he has confidence in his own
integrity and knows that just men will not be forsaken
by their God.

iv. 2. A word, should we attempt, wouldst thou be grieved?
    Yet who from speaking can refrain?
3. Lo many hast thou taught,
    And strengthened oft the feeble hands.
4. The faltering steps thy speech hath rendered firm,
    The sinking knees made strong.
5. But now it comes to thee and thou art weary;
    It toucheth thee, and thou art sore amazed.
6. Is not thy fear (of God) thy confidence?
    Is not thy hope the pureness of thy ways?
7. Call now to mind: when has the guiltless perished?
    And where were just men hopelessly destroyed?

Here we have the revelation that came to him in
visions of the night and the message that it brought
concerning man's imperfection in the sight of God.

12. To me, at times, there steals a warning word;
    Mine ear its whisper seems to catch.
13. In troubled thoughts from spectres of the night,
    When falls on men the vision-seeing trance
14. And fear has come, and trembling dread,
    And made my every bone to thrill with awe,
15. 'Tis then before me stirs a breathing form,
    O'er all my flesh it makes the hair rise up.

16. It stands, no face distinct can I discern;
    An outline is before mine eyes,
    Deep silence! Then a voice I hear:

The message is that man in the presence of his Maker
cannot claim to be just; as the modern poet says,
"Merit lives from man to man, but not from man, O
Lord, to Thee."

17. Can mortal man be just before God?
    Can proud man be pure in his Maker's presence?
18. In His own servants, Lo, He trusteth not,
    Even on His angels doth he charge defect.
19. Much more to them who dwell in homes of clay
    With their foundation laid in dust,
    And crumbled like the moth.

Considering these things, placing the power of God
from whom there is no appeal, alongside of man's
insignificance and frailty, Job should learn that restless irritation and wild complaint are mere folly:

v. 2. Vexation slays the foolish man;
      It is the simple one whom anger kills.
3. I've seen the foolish taking root;
   But suddenly his home was cursed.
4. His sons, from safety far removed,
   Are trampled in the gate, no helper near.
5. His harvest doth the hungry man devour;
   Even from the thorns he seizes it,
   Whilst thirsty robbers swallow up his wealth.

The man who is afflicted should therefore turn to
God, knowing that He is just and that it is by His
wonderful work that the poor are delivered, and the
plans of arrogant, crafty men defeated.

8. To God, then, surely would I seek;
   To God would I commit my trust;
9. Who doeth great things and unsearchable
   Wonderful things without number

11. The lowly ones he sets on high;
    The souls that mourn in safety are exalted;
12. He foils the cunning in their vain device;
    So that their hands cannot pursue wise plans;
13. He snares the wise in their own craftiness;
    While the dissembler's plot is rushed to ruin.
14. These are the men who meet darkness in the day;
    Who grope at highest noon as in the night.
15. So he saveth the orphans from their sword,
    From their strong hand he saves the poor.
16. And thus the weak has hope.
    And foul injustice shuts her greedy mouth.

Suffering may be wholesome chastening, not the pre-
lude to destruction but the preparation for a larger
life and richer experience.

17. O blessed is the man whom God reproves.
    The Almighty's chastening therefore spurn thou not.
18. 'Tis true He woundeth, yet he bindeth up;
    He smiteth, yet 'tis His own hand that heals.
19. In troubles six will He deliver thee;
    In seven—still no harm shall touch thy soul.
20. In famine, He from death will thee redeem,
    And in war from the power of the sword.
21. From the tongue's smiting thou art hidden safe,
    Nor shalt thou fear war's wasting when it comes.

The remaining words of this chapter expand this
thought, promise a complete reversal of Job's present
circumstances; a peaceable habitation and a large family shall again be his, and the real end when it comes
shall be natural and peaceful.

26. Then thou thyself, in ripened age, unto the grave
      shall come,
    As sheaf that in its season to the garner mounts;
27. Lo this, we have pondered well; this is our thought;
    O hear and know it; take it to thyself.

3. *Chapters vi-vii*

(a.) *Job's First Reply to Eliphaz*

In these two chapters Job expresses powerfully the greatness of his affliction as explaining the strong language of his bitter complaint. He may have his faults, but his punishment is out of all proportion to his sins. The sharpness of the trial comes from the fact that God sends these sufferings and the commonplace consolation of his friend gives no real help. It is doubtful whether verse 7 refers to the suffering or to the insipid speech by which he is to be consoled.

2. O could my grief be weighed,
  And poised against it in the scale, my woe!
3. For now it would be heavier than the sand;
  And thence it comes my incoherent speech.
4. For Shaddai's arrows are within my flesh;
  Their poison drinketh up my soul;
  God's terrors stand arrayed before my face;
  My soul refuses to be still.
5. Brays the wild ass when the green herb is nigh?
  Or lows the ox when fodder is before him?
6. Unsalted, tasteless—how can it be eaten?
  What relish is there in the milkweed's juice?
7. (So with your words) my soul refuses them.

Job again desires death as the deliverance from his pains on the ground that he is burdened beyond what any mortal man can be expected to endure.

8. O that my prayer were heard;
  That God would grant the thing for which I long.
9. Let Him consent and crush me down;
  Let loose his hand and cut my thread of life.
10. For here would be my comfort still.
  Yea, I would exult in pain that spareth not.
11. But what then is my strength, that I should hope?
  And what mine end that I be patient still?

12. My strength? Is it the strength of stones?
    Or is my flesh of brass?
13. Is not my help within me gone?
    And all hope of deliverance driven from me?

Job compares his friends to the streams which disappoint the travellers in the desert, who having turned aside expecting to find water discover only the dry channels, and so meet unexpected disaster.

14. He that withholds kindness from his friends
    Even he forsaketh the fear of the Almighty.
15. And so my friends, illusive as the brook,
    As bed of streams whose waters pass away;
16. As turbid floods are darkened from the sleet,
    As on their face the snowflakes hide themselves;
17. What time they shrink deserted of their springs,
    As quenched in heat they vanish from their place,
19. The caravans of Tema look for them,
    The companies of Sheba hope in vain;
20. Confounded are they where they once did trust;
    They reach the spot and stand in helpless maze.

The chapter closes with a direct appeal to the friends that they should show him wherein he is wrong; they pay attention to the form of his wild words and miss the substance of his complaint; he also can claim to have understanding and discernment.

24. Give me your counsel, and I'll hold my peace;
    And let me clearly know where I am wrong.
25. How mighty are the words of righteousness!
    But your reproving! How does it convince?
26. At words do ye your censures aim?
    At wind—such words as one may utter in despair?
28. And now, O turn to me, behold my face,
    I will not speak before you what is false.
29. Return I pray; let not the wrong prevail.
    Return again; there's justice on my side.
30. Is there perverseness in my tongue?
    Cannot my conscience still discern iniquity?

4. Chapter vii

Job continues his complaint, expressing in words full of deep pathos the intensity of his sufferings, the shortness of life, and the lack of any real hope for the future.

1. Is not man's life a warfare on the earth?
   His day, the hireling's day?
2. As gasps the servant for the shadow's turn,
   As longs the toiler for his labour's end,
3. So am I made the heir to months of wretchedness,
   And nights of pain they number out to me.
4. When I lie down I say:
   How long till I arise, and night be o'er?
   Then am I full of tossings till the dawn.
5. My flesh is clothed with worms and clods of earth,
   My leprous skin heals up and runs again.
6. My days are swifter than the weaver's shuttle,
   They pass away without a gleam of hope.
7. Remember that my life is breath;
   Mine eye shall not again behold the good.
9. As fades the cloud and vanishes away,
   So one goes down to Sheol, never to ascend.
10. No more to his own house he cometh back,
    The place that knew him knoweth him no more.

In the following passage Job reiterates his determination to utter complaints against the injustice of the treatment meted out to him. He cannot understand why a frail man should be called to suffer such intolerable pains. Why should the mighty power that curbed fierce monsters in creating the ordered world be used to crush one who at heart is not a rebel? It has been said that Job here, verse 17, *parodies* the eighth Psalm. That word may be objectionable to some, but it is worth while noting the difference in tone and temper between the two passages, and it seems probable that there is a direct allusion. Job admits that God condescends to pay attention to man's life, but to him it is that of a sharp unsympathetic "watcher." Psalm VIII. 4-9, and the contrast, VII. 11ff.:

> What is man that thou art mindful of him?
> And the son of man that thou visitest him?
> For thou hast made him but little lower than the angels
> And crowned him with glory and honour.
> Thou makest him to have dominion over the works of thy hands.
> Thou hast put all things under his feet.
> All sheep and oxen,
> Yea, and the beasts of the field.
> The fowl of the air and the fish of the sea.
> Whatsoever passeth through the paths of the sea.
> O Yahweh, our Lord,
> How excellent is thy name in all the earth.

11. ('Tis so with me) I'll not withhold my words,
In anguish of my spirit let me speak,
And moan in bitterness of soul.

12. Am I a sea, a monster of the deep?
That Thou should'st o'er me watch.

13. I said, my bed shall comfort me
My couch shall lighten my complaint.

14. 'Tis then thou scarest me with dreams,
To fill me with alarm from visions dire.

15. So that my soul even strangling would prefer,
Death rather than these pains.

16. I loathe *my life*, I would not thus live on,
O let me then alone; my days are vanity.

17. For what is man that thou shouldst make him of so great account?
That thou shouldst set thy mind upon him?

18. That thou shouldst visit him each morning as it comes,
And try him every moment?

19. How long wilt thou not look away from me?
Nor leave me till I draw my labouring breath.

20. If I have sinned what do I unto Thee,
    O Thou watcher of men!
    That Thou shouldst set me for thy mark,
    That I should be a burden unto Thee?
21. Why not lift up (the burden) of my sin
    And put away all mine iniquity?
22. For soon I shall be down in dust,
    And Thou shalt seek me but I shall not be.

5. Chapter viii

Bildad's first speech, in which he seeks to justify God
against what he regards as Job's wild and unreasonable
complaints. It is better to accept the fact that Job's
children have paid the penalty of their transgressions
than to think that God can pervert justice. Submission and repentance will bring a renewal of prosperity.

2. How long wilt thou speak thus?
   And like a mighty wind pour forth thy words?
3. The God above—does He in judgment err?
   The Almighty One—does He pervert the right?
4. If so be thy sons have sinned,
   And He hath given them up to their own wickedness,
5. If thou shouldst early seek to God,
   And to the Almighty make thine earnest prayer,
6. If thou thyself wert right and pure,
   Then will he make secure thy home of righteousness;
7. However small might be thy first estate
   Thy latter end should prosper gloriously.

Bildad places full reliance upon the teaching of earlier generations that the wicked cannot have permanent prosperity and that the innocent are not left to
perish in shame. The individual whose life is short
should not despise the wisdom drawn from long experience. Verses 14-19, whether genuine or not, are an
illustration of the fact that the confidence of the wicked
man reveals its worthlessness.

8. Ask now the generations gone before.
   Yea, of the fathers set thyself to learn.
9. (For we are but of yesterday and nothing know,
   So like a shadow are our days on earth).
10. Will they not teach thee, speak to thee,
   In parables of deep experience?
11. Grows high the reed except in marshy soil?
   Or swells the flag no water near its root?
12. In its rank greenness, as it stands uncut,
   It drieth up before all other herbs.
13. So are the ways of all who God forget:
   So perishes the hope of the impure.

. . . .

20. Lo, God the upright never casts away;
   Nor takes he by the hand the men of evil deeds.
21. (Wait then) until he fill thy mouth with laughter,
   And thy lips with rejoicing.
22. Thy haters will be clothed with shame
   While tents of evil men are seen no more.

6. Chapters ix-x

Job's reply to Bildad's first speech. These two chapters are much more than a direct reply to the friends; in them Job dwells upon the various aspects of his misfortune and upon the problems that face the man who seeks to understand the ways of God. He is in danger of thinking of God as a Being of unlimited strength who is reckless in the use of it.

2. Most surely do I know that so it is.
   For how shall mortal man be just with God?
3. Be it His will to call him to account,—
   For one in thousand of his sins no answer can he make.
4. Most wise in heart, most strong in might
   Who braves Him with impunity?
5. 'Tis He who moves the mountains without noting it,
   Who overturneth them in his fierce wrath,

6. Who makes the earth to tremble from its place,
   Its strong foundations rock.
7. 'Tis He who bids the sun, and it withholds its rays;
   Who sealeth up the stars.
8. Who bent the heavens all alone,
   And walks upon the mountain waves;
9. Who made the Bear, Orion, and the Pleiades,
   The hidden constellations of the South;
10. Who doeth mighty works unsearchable;
    And wonders without number.[2]

Job maintains that the contest is unequal; frail, mortal man has no chance of giving a fair presentation of his case in the face of such overwhelming power.

11. Lo, he goes by me, but I see Him not;
    Sweeps past but I perceive Him not;
12. See, He assails: then who shall turn Him back?
    Or who shall say to Him, what doest Thou?
13. (Vain check) Eloah turns not back His wrath,
    The helpers of Rahab bow down under Him.
14. How then can I reply?
    And choose my words (to argue) with Him?
15. I could not plead, even if I were just;
    But to my Judge must supplication make;
16. If I called He would not answer me,
    I could not trust that He had heard my voice.
17. He who o'erwhelms me with whirlwind storm,
    And without cause my wounds so multiplies;
18. Who does not suffer me to catch my breath,
    But fills me with exceeding bitterness.
19. Is it a matter of strength then He is there,
    Is it a question of right who can summon Him?
20. If I claim righteousness my own mouth condemns
    me;
    Were I upright He would show me still perverse.
21. I am guiltless, I care not for myself,
    I despise my life, it is all one;

[2] Some scholars regard verses 8-10 as a later expansion that delays the movement, but they are so well known that they cannot very well be spared from this place.

22. The guilty or the guiltless, He consumes alike.
    If not He, who is it then?
23. Comes then the pestilential scourge that slays so
    suddenly!
    He mocks the innocent in their calamity.
24. Earth is abandoned to the wicked's hand;
    The faces of the judges He doth veil.

Another of those wonderful descriptions of the shortness of life; which is regarded as an evil and again Job
reiterates his desire for the end; it is poetry, not logic,
that we are dealing with. He tries, in vain, to forget
his pains; the thing, however, that oppresses him most
is that, whatever his moods may be, he is treated as
"a wicked man."

25. My days are swifter than the post;
    They flee apace they see no good.
26. As sweeps the light papyrus bark,
    Or as the eagle dashes on its prey.
27. When I resolve my mourning I'll forget,
    Cast off my look of sorrow, smile again,
28. Then with a shudder I recall my woe;
    So sure am I Thou wilt not hold me guiltless
30. Should I wash myself in water pure as snow,
    And cleanse my hands with lye;
31. Then wouldst Thou plunge me in the ditch,
    So that my very garments would abhor me.

The chapter ends with the thought that a man burdened with pains that are a proof of the divine displeasure cannot meet Him in judgment except at a
great disadvantage, as there is no mediator to exert a
reconciling influence. Verse 34 seems to have inspired
G. Herbert's (1593-1633) hymn, which begins:

> Throw away Thy rod,
> Throw away Thy wrath;
>   O my God,
> Take the gentle path.

32. For He is not a man like me, that I should answer
    Him
    In judgment, then, together we might come.
33. But now there is no umpire who can chide.
    And lay his tempering hand upon us both.
34. O would He take His rod away;
    So that His terror might not awe my soul.
35. Then fearless would I plead my cause;
    For I am not so with myself.[*]

In chapter x Job continues his complaint, acknowl-
edging that it is vain for mortal man to stand up against
a Being so *powerful*. Must he be driven to regard God
as one who like a jealous, revengeful man is ever seeking causes of offence?

1. Unto my inward plaint I yield myself;
   O let me speak my soul in bitterness.
2. Unto Eloah will I say, condemn me not;
   O, let me know why thou dost strive with me?
3. Is it Thy pleasure that Thou shouldst oppress?
   That Thou shouldst cast away thy handiwork?
4. Hast Thou the eyes of flesh?
   Dost Thou behold as mortal man beholdeth?
6. That Thou shouldst seek for my iniquity,
   And hunt up all my sin?
7. Although Thou knowest I'm not guilty
   But none can save me from Thy hand.

Job now raises the question, that brings him face
to face with the great mystery, why should God put so
much skill and care into the making of a man who is
destined to be the victim of such a cruel fate? With
this passage the words of the Psalmist should be compared; the subject is the same, but again the tone is
different.

[*] A difficult line variously interpreted, "I am not conscious of guilt
in myself," "I am not myself," i.e., my mind is confused, etc., etc.

Wonderful are thy works;
And that my soul knoweth right well.
My frame was not hidden from thee,
When I was made in secret,
Curiously wrought in the lowest parts of the earth,
Thine eyes did see mine imperfect substance,
And in thy book were all my members written,
Which day by day were fashioned,
When as yet there was none of them.
How precious also are thy thoughts unto me, O God!
How great is the sum of them.

(Ps. cxxxix. 14.)

8. Still Thine own hands have wrought me, fashioned
me;
Afterwards Thou hast turned against me to destroy.

9. Remember, now that Thou hast made me as clay;
And wilt thou turn me back to dust?

10. Hast Thou not poured me out as milk?
And curdled me like cheese?

11. With skin and flesh, hast Thou not clothed me
round?
With bone and sinews woven firm my frame?

12. With life and goodness hast Thou framed me,
Whilst o'er my breath thy providence hath watched.

13. But these things wast thou hiding in thy heart,
All this, I know, was fixed in Thy decree.

14. When'er I sin, Thine eye is noting it,
And Thou wilt not absolve me from my guilt.

15. Yes, woe to me if I act wickedly;
If righteous, still may I not lift up my head;

16. For it rises high, so like a lion dost Thou still pursue,
And still repeat thy wondrous dealings with me.

17. Against me dost Thou bring new witnesses.
Thine anger with me Thou dost still increase,
As everchanging hosts against me come.

With 18 and 19 compare iii. 11, 12.

20. How few my days! O let Him then forbear
And turn from me, that I may be cheerful for a
while,

  21. Before I go whence I shall not return,
       To the land of darkness and deep gloom.

7. Chapter xi

The speech of Zophar, the youngest of the three
friends who adopts a rougher style. He charges Job
with wild words, senseless ravings, and asks him to
stand soberly before God's "mystery," but he declares
that even for the stubborn and rebellious there is hope
in repentance which if sincere may lead to renewed
prosperity.

  2. A flood of words; demands it no reply?
      A man all lips, shall he be justified.
  3. Thy clamours shall they silence men;
      That thou may'st thus rave on without rebuke.
  4. And say my conduct, it is clean,
      I am guiltless in Thine eyes,
  5. O were it so that God would really speak;
      And for thy silencing His lips unclose.
  6. And show thee wisdom's hidden depths
      That it is wonderful in counsel.
  7. Eloah's secret canst thou find it out?
      Or Shaddai's perfect way canst thou explore?
  8. Higher than heaven's height; what canst thou do?
      Deeper than Sheol's depths; what canst thou know?
  9. Its measurement is longer than the earth,
      And broader than the sea.
  11. For well He knows the men of vanity;
      Their evil sees and marks it carefully.
  12. And a vain man will get understanding;
      When a wild ass's colt is born a man.
  13. (But as for thee) If thou prepare thy heart,
      And spread thy hands (in humble prayer) before
        Him,
  15. Then shalt thou lift thy face without a stain,
      Then shalt thou stand secure with nought to dread.
  16. For thy sharp pain shalt thou forget,
      And like the passing waters think of it no more.

17. Brighter than noon shall thy life again arise;
    And what is darkness now shall be like noon.
18. Then shalt thou be assured that there is hope.
    Though now ashamed, in peace shalt thou lie
        down.
19. While many shall then make suit to thee,
    But as for wicked men their eyes shall fail.
20. Their refuge perishes from them;
    Their hope—'tis like the parting breath.

8. *Chapter xii*

Job's first speech in the second series. In scornful
tones and with fierce energy he claims to be as capable
as the friends of reviewing the situation in the world
and estimating the character of God's rule. It looks
as if a number of verses had been added which weaken
rather than strengthen his attack upon the justice of
the world-order.

2. Ye are the people, there's no doubt;
   And wisdom dies with you.
3. But I have understanding like yourselves;
   Who knoweth not such things as these?
11. Doth not the ear try words,
    As the palate tastes food?
12. Does wisdom consist in many years?
    Doth understanding dwell with length of days?
14. Lo! He casts down; it never can be built;
    He shutteth, and there can be no opening.
15. The waters he withholds; the streams are dry;
    He sends them forth, and they lay waste the earth.
16. With Him is power, eternal truth is His;
    To Him alike are known deceiver and deceived.
17. 'Tis He that leadeth counsellors despoiled,
    And makes the judges fools.
18. 'Tis He who breaks the bonds of kings,
    And binds their loins with cords.
19. Priests too He leadeth, stripped of authority;
    And thrones firmly fixed He overthrows.

20. The trusted He deprives of speech,
    And takes away the judgment of the old.
21. On nobles does He pour contempt,
    And renders weak the girdle of the strong.
23. He makes the nations grow and then destroys;
    Extends their bounds, then lets them pass away,
24. Chiefs of the earth of reason he deprives,
    And makes them wander in a pathless waste.
25. They grope in darkness, where no light appears,
    He makes them stagger like a drunken man.

9. *Chapter xiii*

Job reiterates his claim to equal knowledge and wisdom, but it is to God and not to them that he would make his direct appeal.   Let them stand aside, he is prepared to take the risk of challenging the divine judgment.   This he proceeds to do in vigorous terms.

1. Behold all this mine eye hath seen,
   Mine ear hath heard and understood it well.
2. What ye know I do also know:
   In nothing do I fall below you.
3. For truly 'tis to Shaddai I would speak,
   With God to plead—this is my strong desire.
4. But ye indeed! forgers of lies are ye;
   Physicians of no value are ye all.
5. O that you would be altogether still,
   For that would surely be your wisest way.
6. But hear now the pleading of my mouth,
   O listen to the strivings of my lips.
7. For God, will ye speak what is wrong?
   And utter specious things in His behalf?
8. Can ye show partiality for Him?
   Is it for God indeed that ye contend?
9. Say is it well that He should search you out?
   Or as man mocketh man, so mock ye Him?
10. Surely, He will make your condemnation clear;
    If thus, in secret, ye show partiality.
11. Shall not His glory fill you with alarm?
    His dread upon you fall?

12. Pictures in ashes drawn, your maxims grave; *
    Your strong defences are but mounds of clay.
13. Be still; let me alone, that I may speak
    Whatever may come upon me.
14. My flesh will I take in my teeth,
    My very life will carry in my hand.
15. Behold, He will slay me, I have no hope;
    Yet will I maintain my ways before Him.
18. Behold me now; I have prepared my case;
    For I know that I can maintain my right.
19. Who is it that can contend with me?
    So that I should hold my peace and die.

The remainder of the chapter is a direct appeal to
God, beginning with the request that these "two
things" shall be done to him, a repetition of the request
in ix. 34:

> Let Him take His rod away from me,
> And let not His terror make me afraid.

How can he present his appeal and plead his case if
still oppressed by intolerable pains and the mystery of
God's dealings.

20. Only two things do not unto me;
    Then from Thy face I will not hide myself.
21. Far off withdraw thy hand from me;
    Nor let thy terror fill me with alarm.
22. Then call Thou; I will make response,
    Or I will speak, and do thou answer.
23. How great is my guilt and transgression?
    My sins? Let me know.
24. Why hidest Thou Thy face from me?
    Why hold me for thy foe?
25. A driven leaf wouldst Thou affright?
    The withered chaff pursue?
26. For bitter things against me Thou dost write;
    And to my youthful sins Thou makest me the heir.

* Your memorable or traditional sayings are proverbs in ashes,
the fire or life has gone out of them.

27. My feet Thou puttest in the stocks
    And guardest all my ways,
28. So that I am like a rotten thing that consumeth,
    Or like a garment which the moth devours.

10. Chapter xiv

(a.) *The Brevity and Restlessness of Human Life.*
There is hope for a tree that when it is cut down it
may revive from its roots; but for man there is no hope
of revival after death. Job's view is gloomy, but the
fact that he dwells with such sad yearning on the
dreary outlook shows that there is a hungering after
the hope of immortality.

1.   Man of woman born;
   Few are his days and full of restlessness.
2. He cometh forth like a flower, and is mown down;
   Flees like a passing shadow—makes no stay.
3. On such a being openest thou Thine eye,
   To bring him into judgment with Thyself.
5. If now his days are all decreed,
   And fixed the number of his months by Thee,
6. Then turn away from him and let him rest,
   Till like a hireling he enjoy his day.
7. For a tree there still is hope,
   Cut it down, it springs again;
   Nor do its suckers fail.
8. Though in the earth its roots be old,
   Its stump all dead and (buried) in the dust,
9. Yet through the scent of water will it bud
   And send forth shoots like a new planted stem.
10. But man dies and fallen wastes away;
    Man draws his parting breath and where is he?
12. Until the Heavens be gone, they ne'er awake
    Nor start them from their sleep.
13. O that in Sheol Thou wouldst lay me up;
    That Thou wouldst hide me till Thy wrath shall
        turn,
    Set me a time, and then remember me.

14. When man dies does he live again?
    All the days of my warfare I would wait
    Till my release should come.

15. Then thou shouldst call and I would answer Thee,
    For Thou wouldst yearn towards thy handiwork.

16. But now Thou numberest my steps;
    Thou wilt not pass over my sins.

17. Sealed as in a bag, is my transgression bound,
    And mine iniquity Thou sewest up.

18. Yes—even the mountain falling wastes away;
    The rock slow changes from its ancient place;

19. The water wears away the stones;
    Its overflowings sweep away the soil;
    So makest Thou to perish human hope.

12a. And man lies down to rise no more.

20. Thou overpow'rest man and he departs:
    Changing his face thou sendest him away.

21. His sons are honoured but he knows it not;
    They come to poverty, he heeds it not.

22. By himself alone, his flesh endureth pain;
    By himself alone, his soul within him mourns.

11. Chapter xv

Eliphaz, who at the beginning was the gentlest and
most sympathetic of the friends, now, in his second
speech, turns in fierce anger against Job and declares
that with his wild words he has made void the fear
of God; he evidently has wisdom of his own which
pious men must regard as foolishness.

2. A wise man, shall he utter windy lore?
   And with a rushing tempest fill his soul?

3. Contending still with speech of no avail,
   With words that do no good?

4. Nay more, thou makest void the fear of God,
   Confession to Him ever holding back.

5. For 'tis thy sin that rules thy mouth,
   And thou thyself dost choose the crafty tongue.

7. Art thou the man who first was born?
   Before the hills wast thou brought forth?
8. Eloah's secret counsel hath thou heard?
   And kept its wisdom to thyself alone?
9. Tell us—What dost thou know that we know not?
   What insight hast thou, we have not the same?
10. The grey-haired—yea, the very old are ours,
    One full of days beyond thy father's years.
11. God's comfortings—are they too small for thee?
    And speech that flows so gently (to thine ear)?
12. Why does thy heart so carry thee away?
    What means this quivering of thine eyes?
6. I judge thee not; 'tis thine own mouth condemns;
   Against thee thine own lips do testify.
13. That thou shouldst turn again thy rage on God,
    While pouring from thy mouth such words,
14. Say, what is mortal man that he be pure,
    Or one of woman born that he is righteous?
15. For lo, His Holy Ones He trusteth not;
    The very heavens lack pureness in His sight.
16. How much less one that is abominable and impure;
    The man who drinketh in like water his iniquity?

Once more we have, what is frequent in the speeches of the friends, an elaborate description of the certain and terrible fate of wicked men. As this was a favourite subject with those who were confident in their own piety and orthodoxy it may have been expanded.[5]

20. The wicked man is in torment all his days;
    The numbered years laid up for the oppressor.
21. A sound of terrors fills his ears;
    And then when most secure the spoiler comes.
22. He has no hope from darkness to return
    And for the sword he watches evermore.
23. For bread he wonders, saying still—O where!
    A day of darkness, well he knows, is ready to his hand.

[5] For verses 17-19 see ch. xxv.

24. Anguish and trouble fill him with alarm,
    They overpow'r him like a chieftain armed.
32. Before his time it is fulfilled.
    His palm no longer green;
33. As shaketh off the vine its unripe grapes,
    Or as the olive casts away its flower.
34. For the company of the vile shall be desolate.
    And fire shall devour the tents of bribery.
35. Where misery is conceived and mischief born;
    And where the inmost thought deception frames.

12. *Chapters xvi, xvii*

The fierce attack by Eliphaz naturally provokes Job
to strong protest, in which he laments his own fate,
declares that though he must speak he finds in violent
words no real relief. Again he declares that he is the
object, on God's part, of unreasonable persecution. It
seems as if a ray of light would break through
the clouds, verse 19, but that passes quickly and
he falls again into a dark despondent mood. If
they were in his place he might be able to speak like
them.

2. Of things like these, abundance have I heard,
   Wretched consolers, surely, are ye all.
3. Is there an end at last of windy words?
   Or what provoketh thee to answer still?
4. Thus could I, also, speak as well as you;
   If only your soul was in my soul's stead,
   I too against you could array my words,
   Against you shake my head in scorn.
5. Thus with my mouth I could strengthen you
   And not restrain the solace of my lips.
6. Though I should speak, my grief is not assuaged,
   If I forbear what (pain) from me departs?
7. Ah surely now He has exhausted me.
   And shrivelled up my skin—a sight to see.
8. My leanness rises up against me;
   And bears witness to my face.

9. His anger rends, so fiercely it pursues;
   He gnashes at me with his teeth.
12. I was at ease and He hath shattered me;
    Seized me by the neck and dashed me to the ground;
    Then raised me up, and set me for His mark;
13. His archers compass me round about;
    He cleaves my reins, He spareth not;
    He pours my gall upon the ground.
14. He breaketh me with breach on breach;
    He runs upon me like a man of war.

Job bends helpless and hopeless under the repeated
afflictions which he cannot understand; it seems to him
that he is pursued by a vengeance that shows no mercy
and allows no respite.

15. Sackcloth have I sewed upon my skin;
    My horn have I defiled with dust.
16. My face with weeping is inflamed;
    And on my eyelids thick darkness rests.
17. Though there is no violence in my hands;
    And my prayer is pure.
18. O Earth cover not my blood
    Nor let my cry find a place (of rest)°
19. Even now behold! My witness in the Heavens
    Yea, my Attestor in the heights above.
20. My friends 'tis they who scorn me;
    Whilst unto God mine eye is dropping (tears).
21. That He Himself would plead for me with God
    As a son of man doth for his brother plead.
22. For a few years will come and go;
    And I shall go whence I shall not return.

XVII. 1. My spirit is broken within me,
         The grave is ready for me.
      2. Surely, deceptions are my portion,
         And my eye rests on bitter things.
      3. Lay down now, I pray, my pledge with Thy-
         self.
         Who else is there who becomes surety for me?

° Cf. Gen. iv. 10.

6. Thou hast made me a byword of the peoples;
7. My eye is dim with grief;
And all my limbs are like a shadow.
11. My days pass away without hope;
Destroyed are all the desires of my heart.
12. The light of day is changed to night,
The light is near unto darkness.
13. If I should hope, lo, Sheol is my home,
Yea, in the darkness have I spread my couch.
14. To corruption have I said, my father thou,
To the worm—my mother and my sister.
15. And where then is my hope?
As for my prosperity, who sees it?
16. Shall they go down with me to Sheol?
Or together shall we descend to the dust?

13. Chapters xvii, xviii

Bildad, in his second speech, asks if Job is never going to cease his vain speeches in which he assumes that his friends are stupid and that the world should be ruled for his pleasure and benefit. Then follows another of the elaborate picturesque descriptions of the fate of the wicked man.

XVIII. 2. It would be well for thee to make an end of words;
First clearly understand, then let us speak.
3. Why are we counted as the beasts,
And held as stupid in thy sight?
XVII. 8. The upright, sure, will be amazed at this,
The innocent be roused against the vile.
9. But still the righteous man goes on his way,
The clean of hand still goes from strength to strength.
10. But let him now turn back,
XVIII. 4. He who in his anger rends himself.
For thee shall the earth be desolate?
The rock be removed from its place?
5. Yet true it holds; the sinner's light is quenched;
And from his fire no kindling spark shall shine.

6. The sunshine darkens in his tent;
   The lamp above him goeth out;
7. His steps are straitened, once so firm;
   And his own counsel headlong casts him down.
8. By his own feet he's driven to the net;
   In his own chosen way there lies the snare.
9. The gin shall seize him by the heel;
   The noose shall hold him fast.
10. His snare lies hidden in the earth;
    His trap in ambush by the wayside path.
11. All round about do terrors frighten him;
    At every step they start him to his feet.
12. His woe is hungering for its prey;
    A dire disease stands ready at his side;
13b. Thus Death's firstborn consumes his limbs;
14b. And drives him to the King of Terrors.
15. Desolation shall dwell in his tent;
    And brimstone be scattered over his habitation.
16. Beneath, his roots dried up—
    Above, his branch cut off.
17. His memory perished from the land,
    His name is never mentioned on the plain.
18. From light to darkness do they drive him forth;
    And chase him from the world.
19. No child, no seed, among his people left,
    In all his habitations none escaped;
20. Men of the West stand wondering at his day;
    Men of the East with shuddering fear are
    seized;
21. Yes, such the dwellings of unrighteous men,
    And such the place of him who knows not God.

14. Chapter xix

Job replies to Bildad's second speech. This chapter is important in itself and because of the great passage, verses 25-27, upon which so much skill has been spent, and round which there has been so much controversy concerning Job's hope for the future. He resents again the unfair criticisms directed against him, makes his appeal to God but feels that it is still in vain, declares that his separation from God has involved loneliness and isolation from his fellow men. After appealing to the friends for pity, he utters the memorable words, which, however they are interpreted, show a measure of living faith triumphing for a moment over dark despair. It has been said that we could well spare the last two verses (28, 29); but we are not here on the highest Christian plane, and Job admits that his temper is sorely tried.

2. How long grieve ye my soul,
   And crush me with your words?
3. Ten times it is that ye put me to shame;
   Ye are not ashamed to treat me wrongfully.
4. Be it so, then, that I have erred;
   My error lodges with myself.
5. If still against me ye exalt yourselves,
   And plead against me my reproach,
6. Then be assured that God hath cast me down,
   'Tis He that overspreads me with His net.
7. Behold I cry of wrong, but am not answered,
   I cry for help, but there is no redress.
8. For He hath fenced my road; I cannot pass.
   And darkness doth he set o'er all my ways.
9. My glory from me hath he stripped;
   And from my head the crown removed.
10. On all sides doth he crush me; I am gone;
    And like a tree uproots He all my hope.
11. Against me doth He make His anger hot,
    And counts me as His foe.
13. My brethren far away has He removed,
    And mine acquaintance from me are estranged;
14. My kinsmen all have failed,
    And my familiar friends forgotten me.
15. Domestics, maidens, as a stranger hold me now;
    I am become an alien in their eyes.
16. Unto my servant I do call—he answers not;
    I have to supplicate him with my mouth.

17. My temper to my wife is strange,
   And I am become loathsome to my offspring.
18. Yea, even the very boys despise me now,
   They flout at me when I attempt to rise.
19. Men of my counsel from me all recoil;
   And those I loved are turned against me.
20. My bone fast cleaving to my flesh,
   And I am escaped with the skin of my teeth.[7]
21. Have pity; O have pity—ye my friends;
   For 'tis Eloah's hand that toucheth me.
22. But why, like God, should ye pursue?
   And cannot be satiated with my flesh.[8]

The Great Appeal. Job, like other great men who
felt that their experience was of more than mere personal interest, desires a lasting record of his own conviction that God will in some way vindicate the innocent though for a time He may leave them to wander
in darkness. The spoken word is powerful, but if it is
to have any chance of permanence it must be written
in a book or engraved on stone. Isaiah, when giving
a message to his nation which was needed by later
generations as well as his own, said:

> Now go, write it before them on a tablet,
> And inscribe it in a book,
> That it may be for the time to come
> For a witness forever.　　　(Isa. xxx. 8.)

There is variation of texts and difference of opinion
as to whether Job calls for one, two, or three forms
of the record, but the main point that he desires such
a record is clear.

23. O that my words were written now;
   O that they were upon the record graved.

[7] Very difficult expression variously interpreted: "My teeth have
fallen out," "I am escaped with nothing at all," "The covering of
my teeth has shrunk away," etc., etc.
[8] That is: cannot realise that you have sufficiently slandered me.

24. With pen of iron and of lead,
    Upon the rock cut deep.

Many such records have come down to us from
ancient times, carved on rocks, inscribed on tablets,
written on papyrus or skin. Books that seem lighter
and more perishable than the solid materials have
lived on for generations because of the toil of loving
students. The poet never dreamed of this kind of
immortality. He had something to say, and saying
it well, it lives on. We do not know who he was, but
that is not essential, as he represents humanity. The
following words suit the situation:

> All things are doubly fair
> If patience fashion them
> And care—
> Verse, enamel, marble, gem—
> All things return to dust,
> Save beauties fashioned well.
> The bust
> Outlasts the citadel.
> The gods, too, die, alas!
> But deathless and more strong
> Than brass
> Remains the sovereign song.[9]

The translation and explanation of verses 25-27 has
had a long history; both in ancient and modern time
there has been great variety of opinion among scholars.
The condition of the text is such that there is no
prospect of unanimity. The Hebrew and Greek are at
several points obscure; later versions are largely influenced by the thought that here is a clear prediction of
the resurrection both of the flesh and spirit. The
French resting on the Vulgate is clear enough on that
point. "For I know that my Redeemer liveth, and

[9] G. Santayana.

that I shall arise from the earth at the last day; that
I shall again be clothed with my skin, and that I shall
see my God in my flesh; whom I shall see, *I* say, myself
and not another, and I shall behold him with my own
eyes. That is the hope which I have and which will
rest always in my heart." [10] This has been popularized
by Isaac Watts' [11] well-known hymn:

> God, my Redeemer, ever lives,
>   And often from the skies,
> Looks down and watches o'er my dust,
>   Till He shall bid it rise.
>
> Though greedy worms devour my skin,
>   And gnaw my wasting flesh,
> Yet He will build my bones again,
>   And clothe them all afresh.
>
> Then shall I see my Saviour's face,
>   With strong immortal eyes,
> And feast upon His unknown grace,
>   With rapture and surprise.
>
> I know that my Redeemer lives;
> And o'er my dust survivor shall He stand;
> My skin all gone, this (remnant) they may rend;
> Yet from my flesh shall I Eloah see;
> Shall see Him mine;
> Mine eyes shall see Him—stranger no more.
> For this with longing faints my inmost soul.   (T. L.)

From the number of various readings in the Revised
Version anyone can form an idea of the difficulty of
the original text. It would be possible to fill many
pages with alternative versions, some of which not only
fail to find the resurrection of the body, a thought that
is evidently not present, but also by drastic treatment

[10] Lemaistre De Saci.
[11] 1674-1748.

of the text rob it in part of any real meaning, not to speak of noble suggestion. One of the keenest critics attempts at one point conjectural amendation but finds the passage rich in religious significance.[12]

> And yet I know an avenger lives for me,
> A representative over my dust;
> Another arises for me as witness
> Who will then set up his sign.
> Without my flesh I see God,
> Whom I will see for myself,
> I myself will see him, no stranger—
> My reins fail within my breast.   (B. Duhm.)

With this comment:

The certainty here breaking through victorious is prepared for by the fact that the poet whenever he speaks of the death-condition especially in Ch. III goes beyond the usual representation, in treating it as complete non-existence, but it is exactly in these brighter moments in which he expresses the thought that God cannot absolutely desert him, must seek him and long after him when he is away (VII. 8, 21; XIV. 13ff.; XVI. 19ff.) But that was a thought that he gave up almost in the same instant as he conceived it. So far the relative doubt has always gained the upper hand; here for the first time the religious moral idealism conquers. This is the only place in the Old Testament where we learn how the religious (not the psycho-animistic) hope of immortality arises; that it is at first limited to one person and to one moment is precisely its advantage; the hope for all the pious bound up with God, and stretching out to everlasting time is an easier one when once the power of death is conquered. But the two factors which here work together are, first, the need of the moral personality to maintain itself against suppression by an unrighteous

[12] An extreme example is Jastrow's translation:
> Then would I know that my defender will arise,
> Even though he arise in the distant future
> Only under my skin is this indited,
> And within my flesh do I see these (words).

destiny; second, the need of the religious personality to see
God and experience His friendship.[13]

But, again, the fierce controversy must be faced and
the chapter closes on a harsh note.

> 28. If ye say, how shall we persecute him,
>   And find in him the root of the matter;
> 29. Be ye, yourselves afraid of the sword
>   For wrath cometh upon the wicked.

15. *Chapter xx*

Zophar's second reply to Job. He has no new doctrine to reveal; it is a case once more of declaring
that wicked men cannot prosper. They may have a
season of success which increases their pride, but that
can last only a little while. God has so ordered the
world that all things are leagued against the wicked
man. The poor whom he has crushed will see justice
done upon him and his children. As rhetorical description it is effective, but it is not a complete philosophy
of life and does not meet Job's spiritual need.

> 2. To this my thoughts compel me to respond;
>   And therefore is my haste within me.
> 3. Must I listen to shameful reproof?
>   And with wind without understanding thou
>   answerest me.
> 4. Knowest thou this from ancient times,
>   Since man was first placed on the earth?
> 5. How brief the triumph of the wicked,
>   The joy of the godless, how momentary.
> 6. Yea, though his pride may mount to the
>   heavens,
>   His head reach to the clouds;
> 7. As is his splendour, so his hopeless ruin,
>   Who gazed upon him say—where is he gone?
> 8. As a dream he flies, and is no longer found;
>   Like a night spectre is he scared away.

[13] B. Duhm, *in loc.*

12. Though wickedness, while in his mouth, be sweet,
   So that beneath his tongue he keeps it hid,
13. Sparing it long, and loth to let go
   Holding it back still near his palate's taste;
14. Yet in his bowels is his bread all changed,
   Within him 'tis the gall of asps.
15. The wealth he swallows shall he vomit up
   Yea, from his belly shall God's hand cast it forth.
17. He shall not enjoy the rivers of oil,
   The flowing streams of honey and of milk.
18. Toil (wronged), before 'tis swallowed he restores,
   As wealth exchanged he has no joy of it.
19. Because he crushed, and helpless left, the poor.
   Seized ruthlessly a house he would not build;
20. Because content, within, he never knew,
   He will not escape with his treasures.
22. In the fullness of his wealth, his straits begin,
   When every hand of toil against him comes.
25b. He is gone.   Terrors are over him.
26. All darkness is reserved for him.
   A fire not blown (by man) consumes him,
   Still feeding on the remnant of his tent.
27. His sins the Heavens reveal;
   Against him rises up the earth.
28. His wealth to other lands departs
   Like flowing waters in His day of wrath.
29. That is the wicked man's portion from God,
   His lot appointed by the Mighty One.

16. Chapter xxi

Job's second reply to Zophar. At the beginning and
end of this speech he declares that their attempts at
"consolaton" are foolish and false. Their contention that the prosperity of the wicked is short lived;
that their avarice is checked and their arrogance
quickly brought low does not square with his obser-

vation of human life. With verse 14 the words of
Malachi (III. 13-15) regarding the sceptical worldlings
of his day, written probably about the same time, may
be compared: "Your words have been stout against
me, saith Yahweh. Yet ye say, Wherein have we
spoken against thee. Ye have said it is vain to serve
God; and what profit is it that we have kept his
charge, and that we have walked mournfully before
Yahweh of Hosts. And now we call the proud happy;
yea, they that work wickedness are built up; yea, they
tempt God and are delivered." Job here makes quite
clear his difference from the friends; he denies that
their alleged facts are real facts, or if so, that they
represent the world-situation. He indignantly rejects
their conclusion that he is to be judged as a great
sinner because of his lack of prosperity.

2. O listen to my words;
    And let this be your consolation.
3. Bear with me, let me speak;
    And after I have spoke, then mock on.
4. As for me, is my complaint to man?
    And why should I not be impatient?
5. Turn now, behold me—stand amazed,
    And lay your hand upon your mouth;
6. 'Tis when I think, that I am sore dismayed;
    And trembling taketh hold on all my flesh.
7. Why do the wicked live at all?
    Why grow they old, yea giant-like in power?
9. Why are their houses peace, away from fear
    No scourge upon them from Eloah's hand?
10. The issue of their herds is sure;
    Their kine bring forth without mischance,
8. Before them, with them, firmly stands their
    seed;
    Their spreading offspring ever in their sight;
11. Their little ones, like flocks, they send them
    out,
    Their sons and daughters mingle in the dance.

12. To harp and timbrel do they raise their voice,
    In melodies of flute they take delight.
13. In joy unbroken do they spend their days,
    And without long pains go down to Sheol.
14. To God they say, Depart from us;
    No knowledge of Thy ways do we desire.
15. The Almighty! Who is He that we should
    serve Him?
    And if we pray to Him, what do we gain?

After thus describing, in detail, the prosperity of the
wicked, Job while he cannot claim that they are altogether free from suffering maintains that it is the
exception to see merited punishment speedily inflicted
upon them.

17. How often does the lamp of evil men go out?
    And comes upon them their calamity?
18. Like stubble are they then before the wind.
    Like chaff, that the whirling tempest bears
    away
19. (Ye say) God layeth up evil for his sons.
    Let Him recompense it unto himself that he
    may know it.[14]
23. One dieth in his perfect strength;
    All quiet and at ease.
24. His sides are full of fat;
    And moist the marrow of his bones.
25. Another dies in bitterness of soul,
    And never tastes of good.
26. Alike in dust do both lie down;
    Alike o'er both the worm its covering spreads.

In conclusion Job charges the friends with perverting
the facts of real life for the purpose of making an
effective accusation against him. If it were true that
wicked men, and wicked men only, were thrown into
disaster, then it would be quite clear that Job's extreme

[14] Difficult verse or:
    He does not lay up iniquity for his children,
    He pays the penalty himself and knows it.

suffering would be a proof of his great sin. But both
the facts and the conclusions from them were false.

27. Behold I know your thoughts
 Thoughts to my hurt, ye wrongfully maintain,
28. For ye say, where is the dwelling of the noble?
 And where the tent of evil men's abode?
29. Have ye not asked the passers-by the way?
 And know ye not their signs,
30. That the wicked man is spared in the day of
 calamity?
 That they are delivered in the day of wrath?
31. Yet who before his face declares his way?
 And who requites him (here) what he hath
 done?
32. Still to the grave (like others) he is brought,
 And for him o'er his tomb one keepeth watch.
33. On him too, lightly press the clods of the valley,
 And after him come all in lengthened train,
 As countless numbers thus have gone before.[15]
34. How then console ye me? 'Tis empty breath.

17. *Chapter xxii*

This is the last contribution of Eliphaz to the Great
Discussion. He has been the gentlest of all Job's critics, but, here, after maintaining the questionable doctrine that God is not concerned with men's goodness
which is a form of prudence, he charges Job with specific sins (6-9; compare chapter xxix.). As usual, he
closes with an exhortation to seek friendship with God
as the way to peace and prosperity.

2. The strong man can he profit God?
 Nay, he that acts wisely is profitable to himself.

[15] Instead of the last two lines we might read simply, "And every-
body attends the funeral," meaning that the wicked man maintains
his place in society and his popularity to the last.

3. Is Shaddai, then, concerned that thou art just?
   Or is it gain to Him that thou makest thy ways
   perfect?
4. For thy religion's sake will He reprove,
   Or go with thee to judgment's reckoning?
5. May it not be, thy evil, too, is great?
   Thy sins beyond thy numbering?
6. For that thou for naught hast held thy brother's
   pledge?
   Or from the naked stripped their covering.
7. Or failed to give the weary drink,
   Or from the hungry hast withheld thy bread?
8. Yea widows empty thou hast sent away,
   The arm hast broken of the fatherless.
10. Therefore snares are round thee spread,
   And sudden fear affrights thee.
11. Or darkness that thou canst not see,
   Or water floods that overwhelm thee.
13. "How doth God know?"   'Tis that thy thought
   is saying,
   "Behind the thick darkness can He judge?"
14. Clouds are a covering, that He cannot see;
   All by Himself on Heaven's high dome He
   walks."
15. Ah, wilt thou call to mind that way of old,
   Which evil men once trod?
16. They who were withered up before their time.
   Their strong foundations melted like a flood.[16]
19. The righteous saw and rejoiced,
   The guiltless made a byword of their doom;
20. "Then is our enemy destroyed (they say)
   And their abundance hath the fire devoured."
21. O now make friends with Him, and be at
   peace;
   For in so doing good shall come to thee.
22. Receive instructions from His mouth.
   And treasure up His words within thy heart;

[16] For verses 17, 18 see xxi. 14-16.

23. To Shaddai turn, then shalt thou be restored,
    When from thy tent thou hast put far the
    wrong,
26. Then in the Omnipotent shall be thy joy;
    Yea to Eloah thou shalt lift thy face,
27. Then thou shalt pray to Him and He will hear;
    And offerings thou hast vowed shalt thou per-
    form.
28. The thing decreed by thee shall firmly stand;
    And over all thy ways the light shall shine.

XXIII and XXIV appear as Job's reply to the third
speech of Eliphaz. As to the first of these two it com-
mends itself both by sentiment and style as a speech
of Job by the great poet; with regard to the second
questions are raised that are difficult to answer, and
that cannot be fully discussed here. From chapter
XXIV onwards the problem of disentangling the original
from later elements and finding the proper order
becomes more complex, and any result of such analysis
can only claim to be an approximation. Whatever may
be the cause the text of XXIV is in much worse condition than the surrounding parts. After the personal
statement of XXIII, which has been called "a mono-
logue," we have, in XXIV, a description of various
classes of wicked men and the outrages that they inflict
upon their victims. The question as to the use of three-
lined verses also complicates the subject.

18. *Chapter xxiii*

2. Again to-day, my plaint—rebellious still;
   His hand upon me heavier than my moans,
3. O that I knew where I might find Him,
   That I might come even to His seat.
4. There would I set my cause before His face
   There would I fill my mouth with arguments;

5. Would know the words that He would answer
   me;
   And mark what He would say.
6. Gainst me would He set forth His mighty
   strength?
   Ah, no—not that—but He would look on me
7. A righteous man there pleads with Him,
   And from my Judge shall I be ever free.
10. But my most secret way, He knows it well,
    He's trying me, I shall come forth as gold.
11. My foot hath held fast to His steps;
    His way have I observed, nor turned aside.
12. The precepts of His lips I have not shunned,
    I have treasured in my bosom the words of His
    mouth;
13. When He has made His choice, who then can
    turn Him back?
    And what His soul desires, 'tis that He does.
14. The law ordained for me He now performs;
    And many a like decree remains with Him.
15. Therefore it is I tremble so before Him.
    I think of Him and I am sore afraid.
16. For thus it is that God makes weak my heart.
    'Tis the Omnipotent amazes me.
17. For I am undone because of the darkness,
    And thick darkness veils my face.

19. *Chapter xxiv*

As to the extent of Job's contribution to this chapter there is no agreement; all that can be done is to select such parts as are consonant with the general tenor of his speech when he supports his contention that flagrant acts of injustice are perpetrated in defiance of all laws, human and divine. In those days the administration of human justice was proverbially slow and uncertain and the question arises why is not God more speedy and effective in His action.

1. Why are not times reserved by the Almighty?
   And why do not they who know Him see His
   days?
2. Wicked men remove landmarks;
   They seize on flocks they pasture as their own.
3. The orphan's ass they drive away.
   They take the widow's ox in pledge.
9. They tear the orphan from the breast,
   And take in pawn the infant of the poor.
4. They turn the needy from their right;
   All together the poor of the earth hide themselves.
23. God lets them rest in their security
    But still His eyes are ever on their ways.
25. Is it not so? Who then shall prove me false
    Or bring to nought my ways?

20. Chapters xv, xxv, xxvi

Bildad Makes His Final Statement

It is generally accepted now that the shortness of
Bildad's last speech and the absence of Zophar's is due
rather to accidental displacement and transposition
than to direct intention of the poet to show that their
intellectual resources were exhausted and that Job
had gained a complete victory. But the endeavours to
find and restore the original situation has produced a
variety of results. The course adopted here can claim
no special authority; we must find our way as best
we can to the end of the discussion. Bildad seeks,
once more, to explain the situation by declaring the
supremacy of God, who in strength and purity is
infinitely above frail man. The appeal to tradition is
quite in his style.

xv. 17. I'll show thee now the truth; give heed to me;
         And that which I have seen will I report.

18. What sages clearly have made known to us,
    And kept not back—truths from their fathers
    heard.

19. The man to whom alone the land was given,
    With whom had never mingled alien blood.

XXV. 2. Dominion and fear belong to Him,
    'Tis He who makes the harmony on high.

3. The number of His armies who can count?
    Or say o'er whom His light does not arise?

4. How then can man be just with God?
    Or how can he, of woman born, be clean?

5. Behold even the moon hath no brightness
    And the stars are not pure in His sight.

6. Much less a man, corruption's child,
    The son of man—the worm.

XXVI. 5. The giant shades do tremble beneath,
    The waters and the inhabitants thereof.

6. All bare before Him lies the Underworld,
    And deep Destruction hath no covering.

11. Heaven's pillars rock;
    They stand aghast at His rebuke.

12. So by His strength He quells the (raging) sea
    And by His wisdom smites its threatening
    down.[17]

13. By His winds the heavens are cleared,
    The serpent swift on high his hand hath pierced.

14. Lo, there, the outskirts of His ways,
    'Tis but a whisper word we hear of Him;
    His thunder power, then, who can comprehend?

XXVI. 2. But how hast thou helped the powerless?
    Or saved the arm that was lacking in strength?

3. How hast thou counselled the unlearned?
    Or truth in its immensity made known?

4. Of Whom hast thou declaimed?
    And whose inspiration is it comes from thee?

21. *Chapters xxvii, xxx*

Job again takes up his complaint; he is still

[17] Smote through Rahab, a reference to the mythological monster.

oppressed by the thought that God has dealt unjustly
with him, and expresses his determination to hold fast
his integrity to the end.

XXVII. 2. As liveth God who turns away my plea,
　　　　　 The Almighty One who hath distressed my
　　　　　　　 soul.
　　　3. So long as breath remains in me,
　　　　　 And in my nostrils dwells Eloah's life,
　　　4. These lips of mine shall never say the wrong,
　　　　　 My tongue shall never murmur what is false.
　　　5. Away the thought; I'll not confess to you
　　　　　 Nor mine integrity unto my latest breath
　　　　　　　 renounce.
　　　6. My right I hold; I will not let it go;
　　　　　 My heart shall not reproach me while I live.[18]
XXX. 16. And now my very life is poured out;
　　　　　 The days of my affliction hold me fast.
　　 17. By night the bones in me are pierced,
　　　　　 My throbbing nerves (within me) never sleep.
　　 19. Into the mire his hand hath cast me down;
　　　　　 To dust and ashes is my semblance turned.
　　 20. I call to Thee—Thou answerest not;
　　　　　 I stand before Thee but Thou dost not regard.
　　 21. But Thou art turned relentless (to my prayer),
　　　　　 Thou art against me with Thy mighty hand.
　　 22. Thou liftest me upon the wind to ride;
　　　　　 And by the fierce storm I am tossed about.
　　 23. I know that Thou wilt turn me back to death,
　　　　　 The assembly house ordained for all that live.
　　 24. Ah, prayer is nought when He sends forth His
　　　　　　 hands,
　　　　　 In each man's doom of what avail their cry.

Reconstruction of Zophar's Last Speech. There is
no certainty about the particular verses but those that
follow give a clear and final statement of the doctrine
of the friends, taught throughout the discussion that

---

[18] This is evidently too short for one of Job's speeches and may
well be supplemented as above. (Jastrow.)

the doom of the wicked man is sure and swift. This
may be true of some forms of wickedness but it does
not cover all the facts of life, and Job feels strongly that
it does not meet his case.

XXVII. 11. I will teach you now by God's own hand
            How the Almighty rules I will not conceal.
       13. This is the bad man's dole assigned by God,
            The robber's heritage from Shaddai's hand.
       14. 'Tis for the sword his children multiply;
            His offspring are not satisfied with bread.
       15. Those that remain are buried all in death
            And their widows do not weep.
       16. Though silver like the dust he heaps
            And raiment, common as the clay, provides.
       17. He may prepare it but the just shall put it on;
            His treasures shall the innocent divide.
       18. His house he buildeth like the spider,
            Or like the booth of the vineyard watcher.
       19. Rich lies he down, never to sleep again;
            Once opens he the eye, and is no more.
       20. Terrors o'ertake him like a flood;
            The tempest steals him in the night away
       21. The east wind lifts him up, and he is gone
            Tornado-like, it hurls him from his place;
       22. God sends (His bolt) upon him—spares him
            not.
            Though gladly from His hand would he escape.

22. Chapters xxix, xxx, xxxi

The discussion is practically closed; what we have
in these chapters is a longing regretful glance at the
past, the time of prosperity and gracious communion
with God. This lost prosperity is described in detail
and contrasted with his present misery. Then, his own
life and character are vindicated and the way is open
for the final appeal to heaven. The opening words
have often touched the hearts of men who, in hours of

depression, turned from the darkness of their present
position to the happier days of the past. The words:
"A sorrow's crown of sorrows is remembering happier
things" has been used as a motto for this chapter.
We have to remember that we are still in the Old Testament sphere and while there is a sublimity about
Job's statement and appeal the emphasis is still on
the external prosperity which was regarded as the sign
of God's favour. We cannot expect what we call "mys-
ticism" or the inwardness of Christian experience. For
that we must turn to Cowper (1731-1800) the sensitive poet who had his own share of suffering physical
and mental. Probably there is here a reminiscence of
our passage:

> O for a closer walk with God,
>   A calm and heavenly frame;
> A light to shine upon the road
>   That leads me to the Lamb.
>
> Where is the blessedness I knew
>   When first I saw the Lord?
> Where is the soul-refreshing view
>   Of Jesus and His word?
>
> What peaceful hours I once enjoyed!
>   How sweet their memory still!
> But they have left an aching void
>   The world can never fill.

xxix. 2. O that it were with me as in the moons of old,
          As in the days when o'er me still Eloah
          watched.

       3. When shone his lamp above my head,
          And when through darkness by His light I
          walked;

       4. As in the autumn of my days;
          When God still screened my tent.

5. While still the Almighty was my stay;
   Around me still my children in their youth.
6. When with the flowing milk my feet I bathed;
   And streams of oil the rock poured out for me.

After describing the comfort and luxury of his home
Job says that outside, in the city, he was then held in
respect and received willing homage from young and
old.

7. When up the city's ways, forth from my gate
   I went
   And in the place of concourse fixed my seat;
8. The young men saw me and retired;
   The elders rose and stood;
9. The leaders checked their words,
   And laid their hands upon their mouths.
10. The men of note, their voice was hushed;
    Their tongue cleaved to the roof of their mouth.
21. To me men listened, waited eagerly,
    And were silent as I gave counsel.
22. After my word, they answered not again,
    While my speech dropped gently on them.[19]
23. Yes, they would wait as men do wait for rain,
    And open wide their mouths as for the latter
    rain.
24. I laughed at them and they gained confidence;
    The brightness of my face comforted the
    mourners.
25. 'Twas thus their way I chose, and sat their
    head
    As king in the army I dwelt.
11. Then there was an ear that heard and blessed,
    An eye that saw and testified;
12. That I had saved the poor man when he cried.
    The fatherless, the one who had no friend.

[19] T. L. quotes, Odyssey XI, 333, the pause that followed when
Ulysses finished the story of his wanderings:
    He ceased to speak, and all, in silence hushed,
    Were held as by a rapture sounding on
    Amid the shadowy halls.

13. Thus on me came the blessing of the lost,
    The widow's heart I made to sing for joy.
14. I put on justice—it became my robe:
    As mantle and as diadem, my right.
15. Eyes to the blind was I—
    Feet to the lame.
16. I was a father to the poor
    The cause I knew not, I would search it out.
17. So would I break the fangs of evil men,
    And from their very teeth would dash the prey.
18. Then said I, "In my nest shall I expire,
    And like the palm tree multiply my days.[20]
19. My root laid open to the water's breath,
    And all night long the dew upon my branch,
20. My glory constant with me—still renewed
    And in my hand my bow forever green.

The poet certainly knew how to use the force of
contrast to heighten the effect of his speech. After
giving a description of Job's position as a dignified,
respected member of society, who used his influence to
help the unfortunate and to restrain evil-doers, he
gives a vivid picture of "a man of sorrows and
acquainted with grief," a man cast down suddenly from
his high estate and scorned by those who make material success the measure of the divine favour.

xxx. 9. And now their song have I become,
        Yea, I am become to them a word of scorn.
     10. They view me with abhorrence, stand aloof,
         And spare not their spitting at the sight of me.
     11. Since He hath loosed my girdle, humbled me,
         They too against me come with unchecked rein,
     15. All turned against me—terrors everywhere;
         My dignity it scatters like the wind;
         Gone as a cloud is my prosperity.
     25. Have I not wept for him whose life is hard?
         Has not my very soul grieved for the poor?

[20] "Palm-tree," alternative translations are "sand" (R. V.). "The
phoenix" (R. V.) margin.

26. But when I looked for good, then evil came;
    When I expected light then darkness came.
27. My very bowels boil, they're never still;
    The days of pain have overtaken me.
28. Mourning I go, no sunlight (on my way)
    Rising in the assembly, I cry for help.
29. Brother am I to howling desert dogs,
    Companion to wailing ostriches.
30. My skin is black above;
    My bones are dried with heat,
31. My harp, to mourning it is turned,
    My organ [21] like the tones of those who weep.

There is discussion about chapter xxxi, into which
we need not enter, as to whether it formed part of the
original book. In any case it is a noble manifesto of
the morality to which the higher Judaism had attained
and gives an interesting picture of a good citizen.
Besides, it suits the spirit of Job and his claim to have
lived a righteous life, whatever mistakes he may have
made in speech and action. It also forms both a fitting
close to the discussion and a real preparation for the
speech of the Almighty God.   There is agreement
among special students that the chapter has suffered
changes in the arrangement of its parts, but different
reconstructions are offered.   Rigid rules cannot be
applied to poetry in which varied changing moods find
expression, but in this case one would expect similar
subjects to be kept together. These views of what
constitutes sin and of how a member of the community
should treat his fellow members stand in vital relation to the belief in one God which was now accepted
as the foundation of Judaism and to the prophetic
teaching of the past which had given real meaning to
this great movement.

[21] Pipe, or flute, wind instrument.

(a) *General Claim to Sincerity of Purpose and Honesty of Conduct* (xxxi. 5-8).

> If I have walked in ways of vanity,
> Or if my foot hath hasted to deceit—
> So may He weigh me in the scales of righteousness
> And Eloah know mine integrity.
> If from the path my step hath turned aside,
> Or soul hath strayed submissive to mine eyes,
> Then let me sow, and let another reap,
> And let my plantings all be rooted up.

(b) *Denunciation of Adultery* (in the strongest possible language). The zeal for purity of family life and the hatred of immorality is clear, though the form in which vengeance is invited (verse 10) is repulsive to us. "It does not satisfy our ethical sense that for Job's offence his wife, who had no share in it but was another sufferer by it, should bear the greater part of the punishment. That is only possible because the wife still counted eventually as the man's property." [22] Those who have felt the need of apology have explained that Job meant that he would deserve to suffer in the way in which he had inflicted suffering on others. As a matter of fact when punishment came upon a man for such wickedness the woman was exposed to dangers of slavery and appropriation by another man (verses 9-12).

> By woman if my heart has been seduced,
> Or at my neighbour's door, if I have watched,
> Then let my wife for others grind;
> Let others humble her.
> For that my deed of foul intent,
> A sin demanding sentence from the judges,
> A fire consuming to the lowest hell [23]
> And killing all my increase at the root.

[22] Duhm.   [23] Abaddon, Destruction personified.

(c) *Relationship of Rich and Poor.* He recognizes that God is interested in the relationship of rich and poor, masters and servants. In a country and an age where there was so much tyranny and oppression, it is significant to meet with the cry that has fallen from the lips of modern leaders when calling for social justice, "Are they not our own flesh and blood?"

13. My serf, or handmaid, if I spurned their right
    When their complaint before me they have laid.
15. Who in the womb made me, made He not him?
    And from one common mother formed us both?

(d) *Job's Pity.* Job claims that he has shown pity to the poor; protected the widow and orphan; defended the oppressed; he knows that God's care for these helpless ones is real but he is so assured of his own innocence in this regard that he can pray for vengeance on himself (16-22, including 14).

From poor men's want, if I have kept aloof,
Or caused the widows' eyes to fail,
If I have eaten by myself alone,
And from my portion the orphan had no share
14. What could I do when God to judgment rises,
    When He makes search what could I answer
    Him?
He, like a father, from my youth caused me to
    grow up,
And from the earliest dawn of life He was my
    guide,
If e'er I saw the perishing with naught to cover
    him,
Or any lack of raiment to the poor,
His very loins, if they have blessed me not,
When from my lambs' fleece he hath felt the
    warmth,

> If I have lifted my hand against the upright,
> When I saw my helper in the gate,
> Then fall my shoulder from its blade,
> And let my arm be broken from its bone.

(e) *Innocent of the Worship of Money and of Idolatry.*[24] The greed of gain is not confined to any period
or land. "The love of money is the root of all evil"
(I Tim. vi. 10). The other form of idolatry, the worship of the heavenly bodies, had at that time in Oriental lands a strong fascination for many people. We
must concede that it is the highest form of creature
worship (24-28, 23).

> If I have made gold my confidence
> Or to the fine gold said, Thou art my trust;
> If I rejoiced because my wealth was great
> Or that my hand had gotten mighty store;
> If e'er I saw the sunlight when it shone,
> The moon in glory as it walked above,
> And then my soul was secretly enticed,
> And hand (in adoration) touched my mouth;
> Even that would be a sin for vengeance calling,
> For then I had been false to God above.
> 23. The fear of God it was that restrained me
> By reason of His majesty I could not (do it).

(f) *First, the Negative Element.* In these four verses,
29-32, we have first a negative element, which however
is very important, that is, the claim that he has not
rejoiced in the misfortune of his enemy. The desire
for vengeance on those who have wronged and ill
treated us is natural and it finds strong expression in
many psalms: "Let his children be fatherless and his
wife a widow. Let his children be continually vaga-
bonds and beg" (Ps. cix. 9). The view that we are

[24] Cf., "And covetousness, which is idolatry," Col. iii. 5.

to leave vengeance in the hands of God and pray for
blessings and not curses upon our enemies is far
removed from the natural desires and is only obtained
by special gifts of grace and wisdom.   Job claims to
have shaken himself free from the craving for revenge.
It has been noted that Orientals have great ease and
fluency in cursing.

> If in my foe's calamity I joyed,
> Or lifted up myself when ill befell him,
> No, no, I suffered not my mouth to sin,
> To ask a malediction on his life.   (29, 30.)

(in asking his life with a curse, or desiring his life from
God.)

Then there is *the positive claim* to the virtue of
hospitality, which reminds us of the beautiful story of
Abraham who "entertained angels unawares" (Gen.
xviii; Heb. xiii. 2).

> If men of mine own household could ever say,
> That any one was not satisfied from his meat,
> The stranger never lodged without;
> My doors I opened to the travellers.   (31, 32.)

There is some uncertainty whether the land cries out
because it has been wrongfully acquired or on account
of ill treatment to itself; but the antique idea is clear
that the earth is on the side of justice (Gen. iv. 10, 12).
The relation of man to the soil and of both to God
was a living thought in those days.

> Against me, if my land hath cried,
> And all its furrows wept.
> If I have eaten of its strength for naught,
> Or made its toilers pant away their life;
> Instead of wheat let there come forth the thorn,
> And noxious weeds in place of barley grow.
>   (38-40.)

(*g*) *Job's Final Appeal.* He declares that his life had
been open and fearless and that even now he is ready
to meet any charge 33-37. Placed here these words
form a suitable transition to the speech of the Almighty
which in the original form, before the introduction of
the Elihu section, followed the close of this demand.

> If I have hidden my offences from men,
> My sin concealing in my secret breast.
> Because I fear the rabble multitude,
> Or the scorn of the clans affrighted me
> So that I kept silence within the shelter of the
>   house
>
> .   .   .   .
>
> O had I one to hear me now;
> Behold my sign—let Shaddai answer me [25]
> Mine adversary—let him write his charge
> Would I not on my shoulder take it up
> And bind it to me as my crown?
> The number of my steps would I declare,
> Yea, as a prince, would I draw nigh to him.

23. Chapter xxxviii

And Yahweh answered Job out of the storm, and
said: These words introduce God's reply to Job's
challenge and appeal. He has asked many questions,
it is now his turn to be questioned. In the Old Testament there are many appearances of God (theo-
phanies) in connection with storms, especially in
poetry. Elijah, in such a case, meets God and faces
the question, "What doest thou here, Elijah?" and lis-
tens to the voice of stillness (I Kings xix). Ezekiel
receives his first revelation with such accompaniment
(Ezek. i. 4, 28), but nowhere else is there such an elab-

[25] "Sign," in the Hebrew text *taw,* the last letter of the Hebrew
alphabet; it has been variously translated "mark" (Ezek. ix. 4, 6),
"cross" (from the ancient form of the letter), "signature" (R. V.);
"my desire" (A. V.) rests upon a slightly different word.

orate magnificent speech. The storm is in the poet's own soul and God's message comes through this wonderful panorama of the world's vastness and variety. He is not expected to answer these questions but to realize his littleness in the presence of the world's mystery. Personal contact with God and not definite scientific knowledge is what he needs at this stage. First he must meet the unwelcome fact that in the multitude of words that have gone before the issue has been clouded, not cleared.

2. Who is it thus makes counsel dark,
     By words without knowledge?
3. Now like a strong man gird thee up thy loins
     'Tis I who question thee, do thou make known
     to me.

The creation of the earth which is regarded as a vast building arranged according to a definite plan. If Job was there at the beginning he will be able to answer many questions that arise in the inquiring mind.

4. Say, where wast thou when earth's deep base I
     laid?
     Declare it if thy knowledge goes so far.
5. Who fixed its measurements that thou shouldst
     know;
     Or over it stretched the line?
6. On what were its foundations sunk?
     Who laid its corner stone?
7. When morning stars in chorus sang;
     And cried aloud for joy, the sons of God?

The way in which the sea arose and was controlled by God is next set forth. Behind this description are reminiscences of the ancient mythology according to which the sea was a primitive monster that had to be conquered and separated from the earth, the dwelling place of man. In a poet who is a believer in *one* God such features can only survive in a blurred or "washed-out" form.

> 8. Or who shut up the sea with doors,
>   When it gushed forth and issued from the
>   womb?
> 9. What time I made its raiment of the cloud,
>   The thick darkness for its swaddling-band?
> 10. When I forced upon it my decree
>   And set its bars and doors?
> 11. And said, thus far, no farther, shalt thou come;
>   And here shall thy proud waves be stayed."[20]

Has Job considered deeply the daily miracle of the returning dawn and the mystery of light's power and beauty? This is a thing untouched by any power of man.

It is not within our present purpose to attempt detailed justification for particular changes, but a few words on this passage may serve as a type showing how impossible it is to discuss such difficulties in a short outline. Fortunately in this great speech there is much that is noble and powerful. The arrangement adopted from Duhm makes the sense clearer; the R. V. translation is as follows; the clauses questioned are those within brackets.

> 12. Hast thou commanded the morning since the
>   days began,
>   And caused the day spring to know its place,
> 13. That it might take hold of the ends of the
>   earth,
>   (And the wicked be shaken out of it)?
> 14. It is changed as clay under the seal;
>   (And all things stand forth as a garment
> 15. And from the wicked their light is withholden
>   And the high arm broken).

[20] Or "the pride of thy waves be broken."

13b can be explained; the following comment will satisfy many readers: "The fact that the light has the
effect of detecting and dispersing evil-doers is expressed
under a beautiful poetical figure: the earth is pictured
as a vast coverlet, and the dawn which darts in a
moment from east to west (Ps. 139, 9) seizes this by
its extremities, brings to light the wicked upon it, and
shakes them off it like dust." This is well expressed
but it seems far-fetched. The opposition between light
and evil-doers in xxiv. 13-17, a poem describing "the
night-birds" is there an appropriate feature but it does
not fit in well here. While seeking to avoid undue "vigour and rigour" it is difficult to get rid of the feeling
that the great poet would not introduce the question of
the wicked incidentally in the course of his wonderful
description of the power of the Creator. Surely that
has been sufficiently debated. In that case 13b must
be a parenthesis, a form rare in Hebrew, and as Duhm
has said, "the refuge of exegetes in trouble." The dawn
shaking wicked men off the earth is a strange figure.
When we bring 13a and 14a together, we have something much finer, the wonderful effect of the morning
light as it steals gently over the earth creating anew,
as it were, order and beauty. "If we allow Ehrlich's
interpretation 'so that it is reversed as a clay seal,'
improving on a suggestion made by Ewald [27] that
the reference is to the inscription on a clay seal
which is written backward, on being impressed on a
soft object is reversed and comes out in perfect
form. So the sun changes the chaos of night into
order." [28]

[27] Book of Job, p. 301 note.
[28] Jastrow.

12. Since thou wast born, hast thou the morn com-
    manded,
    Or made the dawn to know its place
13a. To reach the utmost limits of the earth,
14a. Transformed like clay beneath the seal.
19. The way,—where is it to light's dwelling place?
    And darkness, where the place of its abode?
20. That thou shouldst take it to its bounds
    Or know the way that leadeth to its house.

The deep and broad places of the world by sea and
land are beyond man's knowledge (16-18, 21). The
latter verse is now generally regarded as "ironical"
though those who regard this as a literal description
of God's appearance on the scene think that "the idea
is insupportable." "The voice of Jehovah sounding
loud above the tornado that burst from the electric
amber cloud; Job and all the rest most probably lying
prostrate with their faces in the dust" (T. L.).

16. To the sources of the sea hast thou gone down?
    Or walked in the abysmal depths?
17. The gates of death, have they been shown to
    thee?
    The realm of shades, its entrance hast thou
    seen?
    (or, "Have the gate-keepers of Darkness ever
    seen thee?")
18. Or even the breadth of earth hast thou sur-
    veyed?
    Say, if thou knowest how great it is.
21. Thou knowest, for then thou wast born,
    And great is the number of thy years.

To us with our knowledge of laws of nature which
regulate the forms of water, the transformation into
the various forms, rain, dew, snow, and hail, it may
not seem to be so great a mystery, but to the thoughtful
mind the mystery has only moved farther back. Here

we have the ancient point of view, the flat earth, the waters around and underneath, the rain, snow, and hail kept in storehouses above the earth. These are all Yahweh's servants, under His immediate control; there are frequent references in the Old Testament to Yahweh's use of them as weapons against His enemies or as instruments of punishment on evil-doers. Long before the modern poet spoke of flowers born "to blush unseen and waste their sweetness on the desert air," our poet laid stress on the fact that God sends "rain in the wilderness wherein is no man," and in these words there may be a hint that man must not regard himself as the centre of the world.

> The treasures of the snow hast thou
>   approached?
> Or seen the store-house of the hail?
> Which for the time of trouble I reserve,
> When hosts draw near in battle strife.
> Which is the way to where the clouds divide?
> How drives the rushing tempest o'er the land?
> Who made a channel for the swelling flood?
> A way appointed for the thunder's flash?
> To make it rain on lands where on one dwells,
> Upon the desert, uninhabited?
> To satisfy the regions wild and waste,
> As well as cause to spring the budding grass.
> Is there a father to the rain?
> The drops of dew who hath begotten them?
> Out of whose womb came forth the ice?
> Heaven's hoar frost who hath gendered it?
> The waters are frozen like stone,
> And the face of the deep is hidden.   (22-30.)

The stars are now considered as separate bodies and in their constellations. "The ordinances of heaven" are supreme examples and wonderful manifestations of nature that are quite beyond man's control. The astro-

nomical details are obscure but the general impression
is clear; in the presence of these great works of God
men should realize their littleness.

> Canst thou bind the clustering Pleiades?
> Or loose Orion's bands?
> Canst thou lead forth Mazzaroth in its times?
> Or lead the Bear with her sons?
> The statutes of the heavens knowest thou?
> Their ruling in the earth canst thou dispose?
> To the clouds canst thou lift up thy voice,
> That floods of rain may answer thee?
> Lightnings canst thou send forth that they
>   should go,
> And say, Behold us, Here are we?
> Who breaketh the clouds on high,
> And pours out the water-skins of heaven?
> When dust becomes a molten mass
> And clouds together cleave?   (31-35, 37, 38.)

The remainder of the Almighty's speech deals with
wild creatures, animals and birds noted for their
strength and freedom; the idea seems to be that even
in their life there are things that man cannot understand or control.

The Lioness and Her Young

> For the lioness dost thou provide the prey,
> Or still the craving of her young?
> When in their wonted lairs they lay them down,
> Or in the jungle thickets lie in wait;
> Who for the evening [29] maketh sure its meat,
> When unto God her children cry,
> (When the young lions roar after booty)
> And wander about in search of food.   (39-41.)

[29] The Hebrew word for "raven" has the same consonants.

24. Chapter xxxix

The Vigorous Life of the Rock Goats

> The goats that climb the rock, knowest thou
> their time?
> Or dost thou mark it, how the hinds bring forth?
> The months they fill, is this thy numbering?
> Their hour of travail, is it known to thee?
> They bow themselves, they give birth to their
> young,
> Quickly they cast forth their pains.
> Strong are their young as they grow up in the
> open,
> And wander from them to return no more.
>
> (1-4.)

The Wild Ass a Splendid Example of Freedom.
This is a very fine description; it is alive with an exultant sense of liberty, joy at the feeling of freedom from restraint. The poet was able to get his parallelism in the first couplet, and yet at the same time secure variety by using two different words for "wild ass." This has caused difficulty to translators who rebel against the tautology; the translation of the passage used here has chosen variety and picturesqueness at the expense of accuracy, as only one species is referred to in this poem. (5-8.)

> Who sent the wild ass free?
> Or loosed the zebra's bands?
> Whose home the desert I have made,
> The salt and barren waste his haunts.
> 'Tis sport to him the city's noise;
> The driver's ringing shouts he hears them not,
> The mountain range his pasture ground,
> There roams he searching every blade of grass.

The Wild Ox is cited as another example of an animal that has great strength but that cannot be made

the servant of man.   The same word is used in the
Assyrian language of the aurocks or wild ox.   "Assyrian
sculptures represent him as a huge animal of the bovine
variety, belonging to a species now extinct.   Tiglath-
pileser about 1100 B.C. regarded it as a great feat to
have killed four of them, and later Assyrian kings used
the phrase 'overran his land like a wild ox' as a
synonym for great destructive power." [30]

> The wild-ox will he be thy willing slave?
> Or in thy stall contented make his crib?
> Canst thou bind him with a cord
> To harrow the furrows after thee?
> Wouldst thou trust him because his strength is
>   great?
> Or leave to him the produce of thy toil?
> Canst thou be sure he will bring home thy
>   seed?
> And gather it to form thy threshing floor?
>   (9-12.)

The description of the war-horse is remarkable for
its liveliness; in spite of two or three uncertainties in
the wording we can feel the movement quivering from
line to line.   For "thunder" it is proposed to read
"might," or "a mane," the phrase "bounding or quivering like a locust" (20) is, to say the least, peculiar.

> To the war-horse gavest thou his strength
> Didst thou with thunder clothe his neck?
> Dost thou bring smoke from his nostrils [31]
> In the majesty of his terrible snorting?
> He paws the plain, exulting in his might,
> And thus goes forth to meet the armed host,
> He mocks at fear, at panics undismayed,
> He turns not back in presence of the sword.
> Against him rings the quiver (of the foe),

[30] Barton.
[31] Ehrlich adopted by Jastrow.

> The glittering lance and spear.
> With rage and trembling swallows he the earth;
> 'Tis hard to hold him in where trumpets sound.
> At every blast he says, "Aha! Aha!"
> Afar off snuffeth he the fight,
> The thunder of the captains and the shout of
>   war.   (19-25.)

Does Job give instruction to the birds so that the hawk knows when to migrate to the south, and the vulture discovers the best place for her nest? Or is there not behind these things and the other wonders of the world the power and wisdom of God?

> From thine instruction soars aloft the hawk.
> And for the land of Teman spreads her wings?
> Is it at thy command the vulture mounts
> To make his nest on high?
> The rock his dwelling, there he builds his home
> The cliff's sharp tooth, the castle's battlement.
> From thence his piercing eye looks out for food
> And sees it from afar.
> 'Tis there his nestlings suck the blood,
> And where the slain are, there is he.   (26-30.)
> XL. 2. Will the fault-finder contend with the Almighty?
> He that argues with God, let him answer it.

This, according to our view, brings us to the close of the speech of the Almighty. That name for God is appropriate here because it is mainly the power and wisdom of God that is dwelt upon. Job has faced a shower of questions, none of which he can answer. Some of them may seem simple enough to us, but it is still true that there are many things in heaven and earth not dreamt of in our philosophy. It is still necessary that the questions of our personal experience should be lifted into the larger light of the great world movement in nature and history. A modern philoso-

pher travels round the world then gives his views on
new things; he has this to say:

There is no actual greatness in sheer physical expanse;
unless it suggests a corresponding heightening of the observ-
er's self-consciousness it does not signify greatness, and
whether or not it causes such a process to be set up depends
upon personal factors. Generally speaking, magnificent
views of nature, such as the mountains, the desert, and the
sea (I do not mention the sky at night because we are too
familiar with it, for which reason it has almost no significance in the sense in which I mean) give a sense of exalta-
tion to every human being. In the face of such a spectacle
our hearts begin to forbode that the limit of our temporal
nature does not necessarily limit our being and that it
somehow depends upon us whether our being is finite or
infinite. The immense forces which we behold outside ourselves, and which we are forced to regard as in some sense
belonging to us, destroy—just as passion does from within
—the armour of our prejudices. Quite unconsciously our
ego expands; we then recognise our individuality as an
insignificant portion of our true selves; we feel ourselves to
be greater, more generous and noble—but also less important and more mean, which in this case comes to the same
thing.[32]

There is a certain measure of truth in statements of
this kind that vary from age to age, but the words of
the poet who felt, though he did not attempt to analyse
the influence of grandeur and sublimity, maintain
their power because of their directness and simplicity.
We may see from his closing words how the poet was
lifted out of himself, humbled but not humiliated, sub-
dued but not crushed.

    xl. 3. And Job answered Yahweh and said,
          4. Behold I am of small account, what shall
              answer thee,
            My hand upon my mouth I lay,

[32] Count Keyserling.

   5. Once I have spoken but will do so no more,
         Twice but I will add no more.
XLII. 2. I know it now, all things are in Thy power
         There is no place beyond thy reach
   3. 'Tis I then who have spoken foolishly;
         Wonders too great for me that I knew not
   5. I heard of thee by the hearing of the ear;
         But now mine eye seeth thee
         Therefore I retract,
         And repent in dust and ashes.

This we regard as the end of the great discussion; it may not be "a happy ending" in the same sense as that of the popular story; "happy" may be used in a conventional, superficial significance that is far from the spirit of Job, but it is a noble ending in which one may find real satisfaction. Job has passed from revolt to resignation. Both of these moods have been glorified by men of great genius, and have at times been expressed in sublime language. That which gives strength and dignity to them is the sincerity of the suffering soul. In the case of our poet, no argument is needed to prove that he was one of those great souls who through the burden of pain and perplexity was led, by frankly facing facts, into a richer experience and a clearer light. Arguments play their part, experience does its work, but such solution as is allowed to us comes through the vision of God.

VIII

PASSAGES REGARDED AS LATER ADDITIONS TO THE ORIGINAL BOOK OF JOB

THE most important part of this volume is the second section, B, where an attempt has been made to present the text in a form that can be read continuously, so that the course of the discussion and the spirit of the great poet can be caught without the expenditure of time and energy on minute and doubtful points of translation and explanation. To have undertaken the tasks that have to be faced by "commentators" would have changed the whole character of the book.[1] Now a separate treatment must be given to specimens of those portions whose genuineness is questioned. While as to the shorter poems there may be doubt, with regard to the longer passages, there is a large consensus of critical opinion.

1. *Chapter v*

Verses 6 and 7 have the appearance of a proverbial saying which was set in the margin and then copied into the text. By a change in the vowels some scholars read "man begets trouble" making clear the thought that trouble comes to man because he is a sinful creature; but it is better to follow the versions and retain the present text. "Sons of flame" is a literal transla-

[1] See the Bibliography.

tion of the Hebrew and has been variously interpreted
as birds, demons, lightning, sparks.

> Although affliction cometh not forth of the dust,
> Neither doth trouble spring out of the ground;
> Yet man is born unto trouble
> As the sparks fly upward.   (A. V.)

> Be sure that evil comes not from the dust,
> Nor trouble grows as herbage from the ground.
> Ah, no! Man's woe is from his birth,
> Thence rises it as rise the children of flame.
>   (T. L.)

Longfellow certainly had these verses in mind when
he wrote, "Resignation":

> Let us be patient! These severe afflictions
> Not from the ground arise,
> But oftentimes celestial benedictions
> Assume this dark disguise.

> We see but dimly through the mist and
>   vapours;
> Amid these earthly damps,
> What seem to us but sad, funereal tapers,
> May be heaven's distant lamps.

2. Chapter viii

(Bildad's speech.)   There is some doubt whether it
is in its proper place, but it is a good example of those
vivid descriptions of the fate of the wicked in which
pious poets delighted:

> The confidence of the fool on gossamer is placed,
> His trust—it is a spider's web.
> He leans upon his house but it abideth not,
> He grasps it but it will not stand.
> Full of sap is he before the sun,
> His shoots go forth o'er all its garden bed;

> Hard by the fountain do its roots entwine;
> Among its stones it looketh everywhere.
> If one uproot him from his place
> It at once disowns him, "Thee I've never seen."
> Lo this the joy of his brief way,
> But (like it) from the dust shall others spring.
> (14-19.)

3. Chapter xii. 4-12

Several scholars regard this passage, in whole or part, as a later addition or as a part of the book that has got out of its proper place; in some places the text is difficult (4-5). The pious man becomes a laughing-stock to his friends in the hour of misfortune, but the tents of robbers are prosperous and peaceful.

> That one is a laughing-stock to his neighbours
> Who called upon God and received an answer.
> The just, the perfect man is a laughing-stock,
> In the thought of those at ease there is con-
>   tempt for misfortune,
>
> It is ready for them whose foot slippeth
> But the tents of robbers prosper;
> And they that provoke God are secure
> Into whose hand God sends (his bounty).

The last line, as here translated, means simply that the wicked are prosperous. Most recent commentators prefer, "They bring their God in their hand." That is the wicked so entirely disregard God that they recognize only their own might as God. Duhm arranges the short poem in three verses of *three* lines each, closing with the words "Who say: is not God in my hand." "Hand" does not need to be taken literally; it is commonly used for "power."

Verses 7-12 are not very clear in this connection with the three statements that certain things are known to the beasts and the fowls, that the ear can test words as the palate tasteth food, and that wisdom is the possession of the aged. The singular "thee" is peculiar in Job's mouth, and the name "Yahweh," verse 9, is unusual.

> But ask now the beasts and they will teach
>   thee;
> And fowls of the heaven and they will tell thee!
> Or the creeping things of the earth, and they
>   will teach thee.[2]
> (Or converse hold with earth, and it will
>   speak).
> And the fishes of the sea shall declare unto thee.
> Who knoweth not by every one of these
> That it is the hand of Yahweh that doeth this?
> In whose hand is the soul of every living thing.
> And the breath of every man.
> (Literally, "And the breath or spirit of all flesh
>   of a man)
> Doth not the ear try words,
> As the palate tastes food?
> With the ancient is wisdom,
> And in length of days understanding.

4. *Chapters xxiv, xxx*

have caused much discussion. The following passages are difficult to fit into Job's speeches but to settle their origin, the exact number of interpolated verses and the precise significance of particular phrases and allusions is difficult if not impossible. It is difficult to resist the temptation to quote a striking passage from the book that is not easily accessible to the general reader. It represents the view that the book is all of one piece and that this chapter is in its entirety a speech of Job.

---

[2] "The creeping things" is not in the Hebrew or the versions, but most recent translators find that the parallelism demands them.

Here Job enters abruptly upon specifications of events showing the disorders that God permits in the world. The whole chapter is a vivid picture of this, although the items are strongly mixed together as though the passionateness of the speaker carried him out of all method. We have here the wretched vagabond wicked, the rich and powerful wicked, the suffering poor, the bold and dastard criminals, the murderer, the adulterer, the thief, characters of every grade, their prosperity and their misfortunes. The flight of the bad man (ver. 18) whether it be the thief pursued by the popular curse, or the fallen tyrant fleeing from the hootings of the proletariat, his rising again to power (ver. 22) his dying like other men, the common grave, the worm, the oblivion, all set before us in a few touches that no effort of Dickens or Victor Hugo could rival; in the midst of this comes the brief-sketched scene of the stormed city (ver. 12), the dying groans, the wailing of the departed spirits of the slain, and what runs through all and affects us more than all,—the thought of God above who sees, yet seemingly "cares for none of these things." This is the polemic aim of the picture as against the friends. Job's darkness has a background of truth, and we need not therefore fear to say that it is better than their false light.[3]

Whoever wrote it, it is evidently a variegated picture!

In the following quotations I have joined as far as possible the translation of the author just quoted with Duhm's arrangement into three-lined stanzas, which at various points is conjectural. Allowance has to be made in many places for the poor condition of the text.

> 5. Behold them! Like the desert-roaming ass;
> Out into the wilderness they go,
> In eager search for their prey.
>
> Without bread they are driven forth
> 6. They reap at night in the field
> They steal the rich man's vintage.

[3] Taylor Lewis in Lange.

8. Wet from the mountain storm
   Shelterless they make the rock their bed
10. Stripped of their garments they go forth

In their hunger they do steal the sheaf,
The oil in strange plantations they must press,
And tread the flowing wine-vats thirsting still.

12. From out of the city the dying groan,
    And the soul of the wounded crieth out for help;
    Yet God regardeth not the folly.[4]

Barton, gaining from the versions the following, says: "No wonder that the text was changed in the interest of Jewish orthodoxy," as Job declares that "God does not hear the cries of distress from these innocent children." But it is very doubtful that the poet placed these words in the mouth of Job, in one form or the other.

From out the city and houses men groan
And the soul of the infants crieth out,
Yet God hears not their prayer.

xxx. 2. Yea, the strength of their hands faileth,
      Men in whom real strength has perished,
   3. Through want and hunger they are shrivelled.

   4. Men who gnaw the dry ground,
      Who pluck salt-wort by the bushes,
      The roots of the broom is their food.

   3. They grope their way through the wild waste,
   5. From human company they are driven forth,
      The cry of "thief" is raised against them.
   6. Within the gloomy gorge their dwelling place
      In holes of earth amid the rocks;
   7. Between the desert shrubs they bray;
      Under the nettles they huddle together,
   8. Children of folly, sons of nameless sires,
      With scourgings are they driven from the land.

[4] Gray. There are several translations of this difficult verse.

xxiv. 13. They, too,—those enemies of light,
Who take no knowledge of its ways,
Who stay not in its trodden paths.

14. The murderer—at the dawn he rises up
To slay the poor—the destitute;
By night he plays the thief.

15. The adulterer's eye waits for the twilight's
shade,
No one, says he, shall see the way I take;
A masking veil he puts upon his face.

16. Through houses in the dark the burglar digs,
In covert do they keep by day,
All strangers to the light.

Seventeen is a very difficult verse, in which the word
"shadow of death" or "deep darkness" occurs twice;
fortunately nothing of importance depends upon the
accurate translation of particular phrases in this poem.
But the students who compare the two English versions (A. V. and R. V.) and others with the two here
given will have another illustration of the problems
faced by the translators. We are thankful that the
preceding verses (13-16) have been comparatively
clear.

Yes morning is as death shade to them all;
For (in it) they discern each one the terrors
of the dark
Light as the bubble on the water's face.
He flees, . . . accursed his portion on the
earth (T. L.)

The darkness have they chosen for themselves,
They are acquainted with the ways of darkness,
Move nimbly even on the water's face.

The passage, 18-24, is possibly a separate fragment
on the fate of the wicked. These verses present many
technical problems and require great ingenuity to fit
them into a speech of Job. Note how, in expressing

this thought, the commentator piles up his adjectives, not less than four will meet the case.

In part at least these corrupt, difficult, ambiguous, or unintelligible verses describe the unhappy fate of the wicked; this is a constant theme of the friends, whereas Job admits at most by way of concession (v. 21) that *some* wicked men meet with an unhappy fate, but only as rare exceptions to the general rule that the wicked prosper. It is necessary, therefore, to suppose either (1) that the verses are out of place or (2) that Job in 18-21 is citing the opinion of the friends to reject them in 22; so R. V. margin, etc.[5]

If, in our second section we have gained an impression of the living movement of the book these questions, interesting to the specialist, are relatively of less importance.

> Accursed is his portion in the earth,
> Both drought and heat sweep him away,
> The melting snows carry him off.
>
> The square of his place forgetteth him,
> His greatness is remembered no more,
> He is uprooted like a rotten tree.
>
> He does no good to the widow,
> Shows no mercy to her children,
> And oppresses the destitute.
>
> Though he rise up he despairs of life,
> Pulled down, he finds no support,
> His destroyer is on his way.
>
> They tower a little while and straight are gone,
> Bowed down they are shrivelled up like mal-
> lows,
> Like the topmost ears of corn they are cut off.

This arrangement and translation, with all the ingenuity spent upon it, cannot lay claim to certainty,

[5] Gray.

but it gives a real sense, whether it is that of the original or not. Three verses from the A. V., where so much of the poetry is splendidly rendered, will suggest to any intelligent reader that this is a desperate situation: 17, 18, 19:

For the morning is to them even as the shadow of death; if *one* knows *them*, they are in the terrors of the shadow of death. He is swift as the waters; their portion is cursed in the earth; he beholdeth not the way of the vineyard. Drought and heat consume the snow waters, *so doth* the grave *those which have sinned*.

5. *Chapter xxviii. A Poem on The Vain Search for The Highest Wisdom.* The counterpart of this chapter is to be found in the Book of Proverbs, chapters I-IX. The subject in those chapters is the practical wisdom, prudence, or good sense which causes a man to choose the path of cleanness and righteousness which is the safe path to health and prosperity. Such wisdom is accessible to man and without it he can have no real success in the affairs of life, so that the dominant insistent exhortation is "to get wisdom."

> Say unto wisdom, Thou art my sister;
> And call understanding thy kinswoman,
> That they may keep thee from the strange
>   woman,
> From the stranger which flattereth with her
>   words.   (VII. 4.)

This wisdom is a kind of common sense that is clearly revealed from the experience of ordinary life, so that it is only fools, "simple ones" or those who are conceited and perverse who can deny its claims or ignore its commands:

> Wisdom crieth aloud in the street;
> She uttereth her voice in the broad places;
> How long, ye simple ones, will ye love sim-
>   plicity?
> And fools hate knowledge?   (I. 20, 22.)

In Proverbs VIII there is a longer, more consecutive treatment of the subject, but beginning on the same note:

> Doth not wisdom cry,
> And understanding put forth her voice?   (1.)

Then description and personification are mingled in verses 10, 11, 15.

> Receive my instruction and not silver;
> And knowledge rather than choice gold,
> For wisdom is better than rubies,
> By me kings reign,
> And princes decree justice

This wisdom that meets the common needs of high and low, which strengthens purity in the personal life and righteousness in the social order, comes from the most ancient times and is of divine origin:

> Yahweh possessed me in the beginning of his
>   way,
> The first of his works of old,
> I was set up from everlasting, from the begin-
>   ning,
> Or ever the earth was.
> When there were no depths, I was brought
>   forth;
> When there were no fountains abounding with
>   water.   (22-24.)
> Then I was with him as a master-workman,
> And I was daily His delight.   (30.)

But this favoured companion of God is destined to dwell with men,

Rejoicing in his habitable earth,
And my delight was with the sons of men.

(31.)

In Job xxviii the subject is the same, Wisdom, but the tone and significance are different. In this case wisdom does not come offering itself to men, they seek it but it cannot be found. Those who regard this chapter as a speech of Job find in it his confession that his intellectual power is not equal to the task of solving the problem of the sufferings of innocent men, the reason being that God reserves such wisdom for Himself. On the other hand it is pointed out that the writer of this poem seems quite content with the conclusion which he states clearly, with fervour and eloquence. Attempts to fit the poem into the discussion have not been successful. The presence of a refrain (12, 20) suggests that the poem may have been arranged on a definite plan, with this occurring more frequently.⁶ The wisdom here pictured, as not only beyond price but also beyond man's reach, has more of a scientific and philosophic colour than what we meet in Proverbs. There it is ascribed to the God of Israel;

Yahweh by wisdom hath founded the earth,
By understanding hath He established the
heavens,
By His knowledge the depths are broken up,
And the clouds drop down the dew.

(Prov. iii. 19, 20.)

Here the fact that it is inaccessible to man is elaborated and illustrated; as it belongs to a later period, the influence of Greek ideas may have been at work. Verses 14-19 are not in the Greek text and so are

⁶ Cf. Ps. XLII, XLIII, and XLVI where in the latter there seems to have been a similar loss.

regarded by some as a later expansion. At the close
a pious scribe has added a prose statement pointing
out that religion is the real wisdom. *"And unto man
he said, Behold, the fear of the Lord, that is wisdom;
and to depart from evil is understanding."*

We are concerned with this selection simply as
poetry and so will choose the expression which while
aiming at correctness runs most smoothly. The R. V.
changes "vein" (A. V., T. L.) into "mine." The
Hebrew means "source" or "issue" and the context
shows that a mine is referred to; "refine" takes the
place of "fine," a necessary change, but "wash out," [7]
we decline even if "the separating process is not by
fire but by water" (x xvi. 27).

<blockquote>

(Where shall wisdom be found?
And where is the place of understanding?)
1. For there is a mine for silver,
   And a place for gold which they refine,
2. The iron from the dust is brought
   And copper from the molten ore.
3. To (nature's) darkness man is setting bounds,
   Unto the end he searcheth everything,
   The stones of thick darkness and deep gloom.
4. Breaks from the settler's view the deep ravine;
   And there forgotten of the foot-worn path
   They let them down—from men they roam
   afar. [8]
5. Earth's surface (they explore) whence comes
   forth bread,
   Its lowest depths where it seems turned to fire,
6. Its stones the place of sapphire gems,
   Where lie the glebes of gold.
   (But wisdom, where shall it be found?
   And where the place of understanding?)

</blockquote>

[7] Gray.
[8] A great variety of translations are offered for these three lines.

7. A path the bird of prey hath never known,
   Nor on it glanced the falcon's piercing sight.
8. The proud beasts have not trodden it,
   Nor the fierce lion passed it by.

It is suggested that 9-11 should come after 5 as they deal with human operations and the transition from beasts to men seems to be too abrupt. We must not expect a poet to be too systematic, but poetry while more flexible than logic runs more smoothly through an orderly course. Verse 24 comes in well after 11 referring to man; in its present position God is the subject.

9. Against the granite sends he forth his hand,
   He overturns the mountains from their base.
10. He cutteth channels in the rock,
11. He bindeth the streams from trickling.[9]
10b. His eye beholdeth every precious thing,
11b. The deeply hidden brings he forth to light.
24. For he looketh to the ends of the earth,
   And seeth all that is under the heaven,

12. But Wisdom—where shall it be found?
   And where the place of understanding?
13. The way to it no mortal knows,
   Nor in the land of the living is it found.
14. The Deep saith, "Not in me,"
   The Sea, "It dwelleth not with me."
15. For it the treasured gold shall not be given,
   Nor massive silver for its price be weighed.
16. With Ophir bars it never can be bought;
   Nor with the onyx, nor the sapphire gem.
17. The glass with gold adorned gives not its price,[10]

[9] Greek, "He explores the sources of the streams."
[10] Literally, gold and glass, etc. It is suggested that glass, though known very early in Babylon and Egypt, may have been rare in Palestine.

Nor its exchange the rarest jewelry.
18. Corals and crystals name them not;
    The wealth of wisdom far excelleth pearls.
19. With it the topaz gem of Cush holds no com-
      pare,
    No stamp of purest gold can give it estimate.

20. But Wisdom—whence then doth it come?
    And where the place of understanding?

The answer is that God alone knows its place and
possesses it; He manifested it in the creation of the
world and the regulating of its forces; He also created Wisdom, or embodied it in the world-order; it is
difficult to say whether it is an attribute, a principle,
a personification, or even a person. The quotations
from a later book given below show that the subject
was treated more elaborately and in a spirit which
blended the practical and philosophical views of Jewish thinkers.

25. When he gave the wind its weight,
    And fixed the waters in their measurement.
26. When for the rain He made a law,
    A way appointed for the thunder's flash.
27. [This verse, whether we translate "it" or "her,"
    seems to set forth Wisdom as a principle rec-
    ognised at Creation and established in the
    order of the natural world.]

    'Twas then He saw, declared it (good)
    And built it firm, and made its testings sure.

may be compared with Driver (I. C. C.).

    Then did he see it, and recount it,
    He set it up, yea, and explored it.

"I preferred her before sceptres and thrones, and
esteemed riches as nothing in comparison with her.

Neither compared I unto her a priceless stone, because
all gold in respect to her is a little sand, and silver is
counted as clay beside her." [11]   That passage reminds
us of certain verses in our poem but in the next, from
the same book, we have something more advanced:

> For Wisdom is more mobile than any motion, and she
> also passeth and goeth through all things by reason of her
> pureness. For she is a breath of the power of God, a pure
> effluence from the glory of the Almighty, therefore no
> defiled thing falls into her. For she is a reflection of the
> everlasting light, and an unspotted mirror of the efficiency
> of God and image of his goodness. And though but one
> she can do all things; and though remaining in herself she
> maketh all things new; and from generation to generation
> entering into holy souls she equippeth friends of God, and
> prophets. For God loveth none but him that dwelleth in
> wisdom.[12]

It is interesting to compare with the treatment of Wisdom in the Old Testament these words of a Hellenistic
Jew written probably in the first century B. C.

The following remarkable passage, on this poem
(Job XXVIII), written from a different point of view,
while it is well expressed has a homiletic if not a critical value. Calling it a "Choral Interlude" this writer
says,

> The controversy at length closed, the poet breaks into
> a chant of the quest of Wisdom. It can hardly be supposed
> to have been uttered or sung by Job, but if we may go as
> far as to imagine a chorus after the manner of the Greek
> dramas, this ode would fitly come as a choral descant
> reflecting on the vain attempts made alike by Job and by
> his friends to penetrate the secrets of Divine Providence.
> How poor and unsatisfying is all that has been said. To
> fathom the purposes of the Most High, to trace through the

[11] The Wisdom of Solomon, VII. 8, 9.
[12] VII. 24-29, Bissell's Translation.

dark shadows and entanglements of human life that unerr-
ing righteousness with which all events are ordered and
overruled—how far was this above the sagacity of the
speakers. Now and again true things have been said, now
and again glimpses of that vindication of the good which
should compensate for all their sufferings have brightened
the controversy. But the reconciliation has not been found.
The purposes of the Most High remain untraced. The poet
is fully aware of this, aware that even on the ground of
argument he is unable to work out the problem which he
has opened. With an undertone of wistful sadness, remembering passages of his country's poetry that ran in too
joyous a strain, as if wisdom lay within the range of
human ken, he suspends the action of the drama for a
little to interpose this cry of limitation and unrest. There
is no complaint that God keeps in his own hand sublime
secrets of Design. What is man that he should be discon-
tented with his place and power? It is enough for him that
the Great God rules in righteous sovereignty, gives him laws
of conduct to be obeyed in reverence, shows him the evil
he is to avoid, and the good he is to follow.[18]

This is very fine as a practical application for ourselves but there may be some spirit of "edification"
also in noting the gradations through which Hebrew
thought has passed in its desire to learn what all men
wish to know, namely, the way to that knowledge
which in its blending of the intellectual and the spiritual deserves to be called Wisdom.

6. Chapters xxxii-xxxvii

The Elihu Contribution. Contribution is a colour-
less term; if we call these chapters an "interlude" it
suggests a dramatic form and an organic relation to
the original book that cannot be proved; the word
"intervention" does not carry us quite so far but it
tends to hide the fact that the intervention took place

[18] Dr. R. A. Watson, Exp. B.

after the real discussion was closed. This is evident
when we note simply that the six chapters run their
course without any external relation to the rest of
the book, broken only by statements that Elihu
"answered and said" (xxxii. 6; xxxiv. 1; xxxv. 1;
xxxvi. 1). What connection in thought there may be
will be seen in the selections chosen. Elihu comes forward to criticise Job and his friends, the appearance
of superiority in his manner and style has laid him
open to the attacks of later critics, but as he no doubt
represented a real current of thought and feeling in
his day he deserves careful consideration.

It is a very obvious criticism, therefore, that the long
discourse of Elihu may be an interpolation or an after-
thought,—a fresh attempt by the author or some later
writer to correct errors into which Job and his friends are
supposed to have fallen and to throw new light on the
matter of discussion. The textual indications are all in
favour of this view. The style of the language appears to
belong to a later time than the other parts of the book.
But to reject the address as unworthy of a place in the
poem would be too summary. Elihu indeed assumes the
air of the superior person from the first so that one is not
engaged in his favour, yet there is an honest, reverent, and
thoughtful contribution to the subject. In some points this
speaker comes nearer to the truth than Job or any of his
friends, although the address as a whole is beneath the rest
of the book in respect of matter and argument, and still
more in poetical feeling and expression.[14]

Though we do not desire to multiply quotations or
prolong discussion, it seems only fair to report the opinion of one who fifty years ago spent so much loving
care on this translation.

Nothing can be more unjust and at the same time more
uncritical than the charge some German commentators

[14] R. A. Watson.

delight to make against Elihu, as an incoherent, as well as forward and impertinent babbler. He does, indeed, seem to repeat himself, but it is his very sincere diffidence that causes it. They are neither affected nor cringing apologies he makes. It is the hesitating feeling of a thoughtful yet modest young man, deeply interested in the discussions to which he has been intently listening, conscious of having something to say which is worth their hearing, and yet having a true reverence for persons, not only older, but esteemed wiser than himself. The introduction and the speech which follow are certainly most characteristic; and if this be proof of artistic merit, it may be said that, in this respect there is nothing surpassing it in the drama.[15]

In dealing with the book, as it has come down to us, it is well to examine carefully all its parts, but our conviction remains that the place for these speeches is *outside* the great poem. We do not intend to make literary style a test of orthodoxy or piety, but it must have a prominent place as a test of authorship. Attempts have been made to reduce the diffuseness, which is clearly recognised, by discovering additions by later poets and scribes. This course has been followed by different methods and to different degrees by several scholars.[16] With this in view we make our selections to show the spirit of this address.

There is no need to repeat here the prose introduction to chapter xxxii; there has been discussion concerning verse 1, where the versions have "in their eyes" instead of "in his (own) eyes." Though the versions are agreed as to this, it looks as if they were mistaken. The idea that the comment of an early scribe who sympathised with the position of the original book has been changed in an orthodox sense seems rather far-fetched.

[15] Tayler Lewis.   [16] See the Bibliography.

There is no contribution to the great subject in this
chapter. It simply introduces the speaker as justify-
ing his interposition in spite of his youth. The preva-
lent idea in those days was that men acquire wisdom
partly by listening to older men and partly by actual
experience of life. This tended to keep the young men
in the background, though they had the consolation of
knowing that if they bided their time their day would
come. Elihu in his impetuosity and indignation
launches his protest against Job, the friends, and the
conventional belief that the older men are necessarily
the repositories of wisdom or the chosen organs of
divine revelation.

6. I am but young in years,
   And ye are very old.
   It was for this I shrank away
   And feared to show you what I thought.
7. For days should speak, I said,
   And multitude of years should wisdom teach.
8. But surely there's a spirit dwells in man,
   'Tis Shaddai's breath that gives understanding.
9. Not always wise the men of many years,
   Elders there are who fail to know the right.
10. For this I said: "O listen now to me,
    Let me too show my knowledge, even me."
11. Lo! I have waited while ye spake,
    To all your reasonings have I given heed.
    Whilst ye were trying words.
12. Yes, unto you with earnest thought I look,
    And lo there is no one that convinces Job,
    No one of you who truly answers him.
13. Beware of saying, *we* have wisdom found,
    (know ye) 'Tis God that crushes him, not men,
14. At me he hath not marshalled words,
    Nor with your speeches will I answer him.
15. All broken down, they fail to make reply,
    (Some power) hath taken all their words.

16. And still I waited, though they did not speak,
    But silent stood and offered no reply;
17. I too would answer, I would bear my part,
    Let me, too, declare what I know.
18. For I am filled with words,
    The spirit within me constraineth me;
19. My heart is full as with unvented wine,
    Like wineskins new that are about to burst.
20. Yes, I would speak, that I may find relief—
    Open my lips, and give utterance.
21. O let me not regard the face of man;
    To no one let me flattering titles give.
22. I know not how to flatter (if I did)
    Then would my Maker take me soon away.

It is impossible to resist the impression of great
diffuseness in the preceding chapter; whether it has
been aggravated by interpolations by a second hand is
not to be discussed here; the beginning of chapter
XXXIII is also of the nature of apology, but is addressed
directly to Job *by name,* a feature that we do not find
elsewhere. Note that in verse 2, the following translation gives a certain strength and distinction to the
two lines which are usually regarded as prosaic in the
extreme.

2. Behold I have opened my mouth
   My tongue hath spoken in my mouth (palate).
   (R. V.)

1. And now, O Job, but listen to my speech—
   Thine ear attentive to my every word;
2. Behold now I have unbarred my mouth,
   My tongue gives utterance distinct.
3. My words—they are my soul's sincerity,
   The truth I know, my lips do purely speak.
5. If thou canst do it, answer me;
   Array thy words against me, take thy stand.
6. To God belongs my being, take thine own
   And I too was divided from the clay.

4. God's spirit made me man;
   'Twas Shaddai's breath that gave me life,
7. Behold my terror shall not frighten thee,
   Nor heavy shall my hand upon thee press.

After this appeal, which has a certain patronising
tone that one would not expect from a modest young
man, Elihu charges Job with claiming to be innocent,
with bringing accusations against God, and complain-
ing that God does not speak in answer to his prayers.
Elihu affirms that God does speak to men "in dreams,
in visions of the night" (15),[17] and if this does not
meet the case he sends severe discipline. But this suffering is an act of mercy meant as a warning to save
the man from utter destruction.

17. To restrain man from his wickedness
    And cut away from him his pride.
18. That from the pit he may keep back his soul,
    His life from passing on into Sheol.
19. With anguish is he chastened on his bed,
    His every bone a never-ceasing pain.
20. So that his very life abhorreth bread,
    His appetite rejects the once loved food,
21. His flesh from sight it wastes away;
    His bones laid bare, before concealed from
    view,
22. Unto perdition draweth nigh his soul;
    His life awaits the messengers of death.

The speech, so far, has been on similar lines to those
of the friends in depicting severe sufferings, as chastisement, and declaring that there is hope for the man
who repents. The illustration is, however, carried to
the limit, to the very gates of death. The word rendered "messengers of death" in verse 22 has caused
much discussion. Some follow the versions and, by a

[17] Cf. Eliphas IV. 13.

different spacing of the letters, translate "to death," others, taking it as the causative of the verb "to die" translate "the slayers," or "the angels of death." If this is an allusion to the angels of death who take the dying man to his place in Sheol it would tend to show the late date of this speech; but, as it stands alone in the Old Testament and is, in any case doubtful, dogmatism is out of place. In later Jewish literature angels with these duties, "angels of the Lord and of Satan" are described as meeting the good man or wicked man in the solemn hour. The same difficulty follows us into the next two verses (23, 24), dividing both earlier and later expositors. On the one side the intercessor is an angel in the supernatural sense who acts as a prophet, and there were thousands prepared for these duties, sufficient to meet the needs of all. The other is that the messenger is a man, perhaps Elihu himself, who is privileged to bear a message to the sufferer that leads him to repentance and prayer, so that he finds favour in the sight of God. On either view the lesson is that if chastisement is rightly received, and so does its work, there is hope, even at the last, for the penitent.

> 23. And is there then an angel on his side,
>   The interceding one—of thousands chief—
>   To make it known to man His righteousness;
> 24. So does He show him grace and say,
>   "Deliver him from going down to death,
>   A ransom I have found,"
> 25. Moist as in childhood grows his flesh again
>   And to his youthful day does he return.

After his restoration the man prays and God accepts his prayer, he sings joyfully in the presence of his fellow men, makes public confession of his wandering

and tells of the forgiveness and restoration he has
received. Then the chapter closes with the application
of this teaching to Job's case.

> 29. Behold! in all these ways, so dealeth God,
>   Time after time, and times again, with men.
> 30. His soul to rescue from the grave,
>   That he might see to the full the light of life.
> 31. Attend, O Job, give ear to me;
>   Be still that I may speak;
> 32. If thou hast words, then answer me;
>   Speak out, my wish is thy defence.
> 33. If not, then give to me thine ear;
>   Be still, if I may wisely counsel thee.

To this there is no reply from Job, and Elihu continues his address, appealing to "the wise" and then
bringing sharp accusations against Job. According to
Elihu, Job has sufficiently proved his own wickedness
by suggesting that God can do wrong. In the charges
against Job (chapter xxxiv) there are several points
of contact with the reproofs of Eliphaz (xv. 16; xxii.
13b). The chapter may have been enlarged (28-33
are lacking in the original Greek version) and have
suffered dislocations.

> 2. Hear, O ye wise, my words;
>   Ye knowing ones give me your ear.
> 3. It is the ear that trieth speech,
>   As the palate tastes food.
> 4. Let us then make the righteous choice,
>   And aim to know between us what is good.
> 5. For Job saith, "I am innocent;
>   'Tis God who puts away my cause.
> 6. Against my right shall I speak what is false
>   (or, Notwithstanding my right I am in pain)
>   Sore is my wound, but from no crime of mine!"
> 7. Where is the mighty man like Job?
>   Who drinketh scorning down like water;

8. Who joins the malefactor's band,
   And walks the ways of wicked men?
9. For he has said: "It does no good to man
   That he should take delight in God."

The simple answer to all Job's wild complaints is that God can do no wrong; it is sheer impiety to attempt to call him to account.

12. Yea, verily, God will not do the wrong;
    The Almighty One cannot pervert the right.
13. Who gave to Him the charge of earth,
    And (upon him) laid the whole world?
14. If He cause His spirit to return to Himself,
    And gather to Himself his breath,
15. All flesh together would expire,
    And man go back to dust.

In what remains of this chapter there are many difficulties in the way of exact translations and clear interpretation. God, we are told, makes short work of the wicked men or nations, and is no respecter of place or power.

22. No darkness is there, yea, no thick gloom,
    Where men of evil deeds can hide themselves.
23. He needeth no repeated scrutiny
    When man to God in judgment comes.
24. He breaks the strong in ways we cannot trace;
    And setteth others in their stead.
25. To this end knoweth He their works.
    He overturns them in the night—they're crushed.

The address then is concluded in the same vein in which it began,

34. Let men of understanding say,
    Or any strong and wise who hears me now,
35. Job speaks in ignorance,
    And without understanding are his words.

36. O would that Job were proved to the extreme,
      For his replies like those of evil men.
37. For sure he adds rebellion to his sin;
      And still against God doth multiply his words.

Chapter xxxv is short and in the central part there
is much difficulty in interpretation, owing either to
lack of clearness on the part of the writer or the poor
condition of the text.

Job (verses 1-3) is charged with claiming to be
"more righteous than God" and with making the sceptical enquiry: "What advantage will he have from his
righteousness," or "What profit have I more than from
my sin?" That scarcely seems fair to Job but Elihu
has the answer ready:

4. I answer thee;
      And Thy companions with thee:
5. Look to the heavens and see;
      Behold the skies so high above thy head.
6. If thou hast sinned, what doest thou to Him?
      If many are thy sins, what doest thou to Him?
7. If thou art just, what givest thou to Him?
      What profit from thy hand does he receive?
8. To me just like thyself pertains thy wrong;
      To a son of man thy righteousness.

The variety of interpretations adopted for 9-13
shows that something has gone wrong with the text.
The different lines can be translated but the trouble is
with their relation to each other. Who are those suffering from oppressions (9) and what is meant by saying that God does not hear their cry "because of the
pride of evil men"? The suggestion adopted here that
9 and 12 are additions and 16 should follow 8 (Duhm)
is only one of several but it yields an intelligible statement.

16. Yet Job fills his mouth with vanity,
    And without understanding multiplies words.
10. And saith not, "Where is my maker, God;
    Who in the night time giveth songs of praise?
    Who teacheth us beyond the beasts of earth,
    And makes us wiser than the birds of heaven."
13. For God will not hear vanity,
    Nor will the Almighty hold it in regard.
14. Yet, even when thou sayest, thou seest Him
    not,
    There is judgment still before Him—therefore
    wait.
    (or, Be still before Him and wait for Him).

It is likely that the words, xxxvi. 1, "Elihu also continued and said," are a scribal note in the wrong place and that xxxvi. 2 is to be closely connected with xxxv. 15, and Elihu goes on to make the suggestion that "God does not strictly visit iniquity or concern Himself about transgressions." He thinks he can make an effective apology—he has still some "words for God," i.e. on "God's behalf."

xxxvi. 2. A moment wait that I may show thee still
          That there are words for God.
       3. I will bring my knowledge from afar
          'Tis to my Maker I ascribe the right.
       4. Indeed, there is no dissembling in my word,
          One that is perfect in knowledge stands before
          thee.
       5. Behold God rejecteth those hardened in their
          heart.
      6a. He will not keep the wicked alive.
      7a. His eye He takes not from the righteous man,
      6b. And justice He will render to the oppressed.
       7. And with kings upon the throne
          He makes them sit in glory, raised on high.
       8. Again when bound in iron chains,
          And held in sorrow's bands.

9. .Then showeth He to them what they have
   done,
      Their oversteppings, how they've walked in
      pride,
10. Thus openeth He their ear to discipline,
      And warns them that from evil they turn back.
11. If they will listen and obey,
      Then shall they spend their days in good.
12. If not, they must pass away to Sheol
      And die without knowledge.

Then Elihu describes the fate of those who persist
in wickedness and warns Job against the terrible and
irrevocable doom of those who neglect or despise the
gentler intimations of God's displeasure. Next there
are eloquent passages on the text: "Lo, God is great,
we know Him not; unsearchable the number of His
years" (26). One of the strongest arguments against
these speeches, as having any real place in the original
book, is that in this latter part they anticipate the
speech of the Almighty which was meant to close the
discussion. It is highly probable that it (or they if
more than one) was written by some one who had
studied the book in its early form. There is general
agreement among recent students that the incoherence
is caused, in part, by interpolations or displacements,
but there is difference of opinion as to how far this
can now be remedied and the extent to which the
Greek and Sahidic versions are to be accepted as reliable guides. First we have Elihu's address on God's
greatness as seen in the world of nature, and then
a poem, perhaps of different origin, on the rain-
storm.[18]

[18] The arrangement of the verses in these two passages is according to Barton's reconstruction.

XXXVI. 25. All men may see it,
           Man beholdeth it from afar.
       27a. For He restraineth the drops of water,
       28b. His clouds o'ershadows many men,
  (or, 27. He draws the drops from the sea,
           And filters the rain from the mist,
       28. Wherewith the skies pour down,
           And drop upon many men.)
       33. (Yet) He appointeth a time for cattle,
           They know the place of their lying down.

XXXVII. 1. At this also my heart trembleth,
           And is moved out of its place.
        5b. Great things He doeth which we do not under-
           stand.
           For to the snow He saith, Be thou upon the
           earth,
        7. He sealeth up the hand of every man,
           That all men may recognise His work.
        8. There go the beasts, each to his hiding place,
           And in their dens abide.
        9. Out of the chamber cometh the whirlwind,
           And from the granaries the cold,
           (The storm comes from the chambers of the
           south,
           The cold from the stars of the north).
        10. From God's own breath the frost is given,
           By it the waters' breadth is firmly bound.
     12c, d. All this does He command,
           On the face of the habitable earth.

Poem on the Rain-Storm

XXXVI. 26. Behold God is great, we know Him not;
           The number of His years is unsearchable.
       27b. He poureth out rain from the mist,
       28a. Which the skies pour down,
        29. Who then can understand the spreading of the
           clouds,
           The thunderings of His pavilion.

30. Behold upon it He spreads His light,
    (or, Behold around Him He spreadeth His
    mist)
    He covers the top of the mountains.
31. For by them He cares for the peoples,
    And giveth food in rich supply.
    O'er His hands the lightning doth He wrap,
    And giveth it commandment where to strike.

XXXVII. 2. Hear, Ye, O hear the roaring of His voice,
    And the deep reverberation of His mouth.
3. As under all the heavens He sends it forth,
    His lightning to the edges of the earth.
4. Then after it resounds a voice,
    The glorious voice with which He thundereth.
    He stayed them not when His voice is heard,
    The rain and His mighty storm.
11. Yea, He loadeth the thick cloud with lightning,
    The thin light-breaking cloud He scattereth.
12a, b. In circling changes it is moved about,
    Doing its work by His guidance,

The Close of the Elihu Speeches

The re-arrangements and emendations proposed by specialists vary in their measure of probability. They assume correctly that a writer of Hebrew poetry, even if not a man of great genius, wrote in a simple, straightforward manner, and that, as he was dealing with the common objects of sight and sound and not with scientific investigations or philosophical speculation, except in the case of rare words, translations should not be difficult. Variety is possible even when the text is clear as the following specimens show. XXXVII. 17, "When the earth is still by reason of the south wind." "Before the south (winds) glow the earth lies still." "When the earth is hushed in the south wind," "When

from the south the land in sultry stillness rests,"
"When the earth is still because of the south wind."
The question of reproducing the poetic spirit as well
as the exact sense of an ancient poem will always be
a living one. Job is now called to consider the works
of God in the heavens:

xxxvii. 14. O Job! give ear to this;
      Be still and contemplate God's wondrous
      works.
    15. Knowest thou how God ordains His works
      And causeth the light of His cloud to shine
      forth?
    16. Knowest thou the poisings of the clouds,
      The wondrous works of Him whose knowledge
      knows no bounds?
    17. (Or how it is) what time thy robes are warm,
      When from the south the land in sultry still-
      ness rests.
    18. Dost thou with Him spread out the skies,
      So strong,—so like a molten mirror smooth?
    19. O teach us what to say to Him!
      Because of darkness we cannot order our speech
      aright.
    20. Should it be told to Him that I would speak,
      If a man speak, surely he shall be swallowed up.

It can scarcely be said that Elihu makes a brilliant
ending to his speeches. The words, in themselves, are
simple enough, but the connection of thought is not
clear. The wonder of the skies and the splendour of
the Northern Lights speak of God's majesty, but men
cannot find him out; it is sufficient to know that He is
perfect in righteousness and pays no attention to those
who think themselves wise.

    21a. Then when men do not see the light,
    21c. The wind passes over and makes it clear,

22. From the North it leaves a golden sheen,
21b. Bright shines it in the heavens.
22. O, with Eloah there is awful majesty.
23. The Almighty One we cannot find him,
   So great in strength and justice.
   He will not violate righteousness.
24. For this should men hold Him in reverence,
   For *He regardeth not* the wise of heart.

Behemoth and Leviathan

It is now generally accepted that these two
animals, described here for the purpose of magni-
fying the power of God, are the hippopotamus
and the crocodile, though attempts have been
made to revive the ancient Jewish interpretation
that they are mythical monsters (XLI. 19-21). With
these discussions we are not concerned here. Whether
it is possible to save a part of this poetry for the genuine speech of the Almighty, for example XLI. 1-11,
where the *question* form rather than the *descriptive*
prevails, must be left to the critical commentator. We
regard these poems as interesting additions that
have no connection with the problem of the original
book. They are simply additional illustrations of
God's power in creation. In them there may be a
large use of poetic licence and the literary quality
may be on a lower plane, but the wonder and enthusiasm about strange wild animals is a thing that we
have all known in our childhood and which it would
be a pity to lose altogether. The zoological gardens
and the menagerie still have a place in our life since
we cannot all travel in foreign lands to see these wonderful creatures in their own homes. As there is no
question of doctrine involved but rather the need of
a translation that kindles in us, by its picturesque fea-

tures, something of the simple enthusiasm and even exaggeration of the Jewish poet who centuries ago marvelled at the wonderful creatures that God had given to Egypt, I have kept as close as possible to Dr. Lewis' version, "Grass, like the ox, doth he eat" represents the Hebrew exactly; "Just like the peaceful ox he eateth grass," suggests the astonishment that such a powerful animal should be content with the diet of the domesticated ox.

XL. 15. Behold now Behemoth,
       (which I made)[19] with thee,
       Just like the peaceful ox he eateth grass.

    16. Behold what might is in his loins;
       The muscles of his belly, these his strength.

    17. Like to a cedar waveth he his tail,
       Whilst woven firm the sinews of his thighs.

    18. His bones are tubes of brass,
       His limbs like iron bars.

    19. Chief is he of the ways of God;
       He was made to be ruler of his fellows.

    20. And yet the hills his pasturage;
       Whilst round him sport the beasts of the field.

    21. Beneath the lotus trees lies he down to rest;
       In covert of the reed—the (cooling) fen.

    22. They weave for him his shade,
       Whilst round him spread the willows of the stream,

    23. Lo, the flood swells, he startles not;
       Fearless although a Jordan dash against his mouth.

XLI. 9. Behold the hope (of taking him) is vain;
       Yea at the very sight is one cast down;

    10. There is none so desperate to stir him up,
       Before Me then (his Maker) who shall stand.
       (or, who then is he that can stand before him.)

XLI. 1. With a hook canst thou draw out Leviathan?
       Or with a line press down his tongue?

[19]Lacking in the Greek.

2. A rush branch through his nostrils canst thou
   place?
   Or with the thorny spine bore through his nose?
3. Will he make many prayers to thee?
   Or will he say soft things to thee?
4. Or with thee will he make a covenant?
   That thou shouldst take him for thy slave forever?
5. Wilt thou sport with him as with a bird?
   Or bind him (as a plaything) for thy maidens?
6. The caravans, will they make trade for him?
   And then retail him to the Canaanites.
7. With barbed irons canst thou fill his skin?
   His head with fishing spears?
8. Attempt to lay thy hand upon him,
   Think of the battle—do so no more.
13. His coat of mail, who hath uncovered its face?
    The doubling of his jaws, who can enter there?
14. The doors that shut his face, who opens them?
    The circuits of his teeth—how terrible!
15. 'Tis a proud sight, the grooves that form his
    shield
    Each one a seal shut close and firmly bound;
16. So near do they to one another join;
    The very wind between them cannot pass.
18. His sneezings sparkle with light;
    His eyes are like the eyelids of the dawn.
19. Forth from his mouth go burning lamps.
    And sparks of fire set free.
20. Out of his nostrils goeth forth a smoke.
    As from a caldron blown or seething pot.
21. His breath enkindleth coals,
    A tongue of flame seems issuing from his
    mouth.
22. Strength dwelleth even in his neck,
    Before him (as a courier) terror runs.
23. His fleshy folds how firmly do they cleave,
    Hard bound upon him, all unmovable,
24. His heart is molten as a stone.
    Yea, like the nether millstone petrified,

25. When he rises up the leaders are dismayed.
    The watchers of the river are driven to dismay.
26. Though one may reach him with the sword it
      holdeth not,
    Nor spear avails, nor dart, nor pointed shaft,
27. The iron he esteems as straw,
    The brass as brittle wood.
28. The archer cannot make him flee;
    Slingstones are turned to chaff.
29. The heavy club is counted as a reed,
    He scorns the rushing of the javelins,
30. Sharp potsherds are his underparts,
    A threshing drag he spreads upon the mire.
31. Like a caldron causes he the deep to foam,
    And like an ointment pot, the Nile.
32. Behind he makes a sparkling path to shine,
    One takes the water flood for hoary hair.
33. On earth there is not his like,
    Created without fear.
34. On all high things he looketh (fearlessly)
    (Or, Everyone that is high feareth him)
    Himself the King o'er all the sons of pride.

BRIEF BIBLIOGRAPHY

Lange's Commentary (Scribner, Armstrong and Co. New York, 1874), containing a translation of Dr. Zöckler's commentary, a rhythmical version by Dr. Tayler Lewis and an Introduction to The Poetical Books by Dr. P. Schaff is a wonderful treasury of information on the Hebrew language, the nature of Old Testament Poetry and the history of the criticism and exegesis of this particular book. We are glad to be able to use to such a large extent the rhythmical version contained in it. Of recent translations those of Drs. McFadyen and Moffatt may be mentioned as well as "An American Translation."

For the student of Hebrew there is now available *The International Critical Commentary* by Drs. S. R. Driver and G. B. Gray, Vol. I, 376 pp, Introductions, Translation and Notes. This is supplemented by Vol. II devoted entirely to Philological Notes.

In Dillon's *The Sceptics of the Old Testament* (Isbister & Co., 1895), following the shorter Greek Version and Bickell's Metrical Theory, the Discussion is reduced to 309 four-lined stanzas, "A Sceptical Symposium."

M. Jastrow, Jr. (J. B. Lippincott, 1920, 369 pp.), a stimulating discussion of the origin and structure of book of Job with radical results.

The Book of Job by Buttenwieser (The Macmillan Company) a critical study and reconstruction of the text by a Jewish scholar.

Commentary by J. Strahan (T. & T. Clark). A careful and reliable piece of work by a scholar who is familiar with the best literature on the subject. In these commentaries lists of books by German and French scholars may be found. Of these B. Duhm and K. Budde may be mentioned here.

The general reader may find stimulus and help from such books as the following, which are not formal commentaries: R. L. Watson, *Expositor's Bible;* Cheyne's *Job and Solomon;* Bradley's *Lectures;* McFadyen's *Problem of Pain;* Sir G. A. Smith's article in *The Legacy of Israel* (Oxford), "Job" in Cassells' *Study Bible.*

Date Due

DEC 1 9			
MAY 1 9			
MAY 2 1			